EMPIRICAL METHODS FOR THE STUDY OF LABOR FORCE DYNAMICS

KENNETH I WOLPIN

Routledge
Taylor & Francis Group

LONDON AND NEW YORK

First published in 1995 by
Harwood Academic Publishers GmbH

Reprinted in 2001 by
Routledge
2 Park Square, Milton Park, Abingdon, Oxfordshire OX14 4RN
Simultaneously published in the USA and Canada by Routledge
711 Third Avenue, New York, NY 10017

Routledge is an imprint of the Taylor & Francis Group

Transferred to digital print 2003

First issued in paperback 2013

The publishers have made every effort to contact authors/copyright holders
of the works reprinted in *Harwood Fundamentals of Pure & Applied Economics*.
This has not been possible in every case, however, and we would welcome
correspondence from those individuals/companies we have been unable to
trace.

These reprints are taken from original copies of each book. in many cases
the condition of these originals is not perfect. the publisher has gone to
great lengths to ensure the quality of these reprints, but wishes to point
out that certain characteristics of the original copies will, of necessity, be
apparent in reprints thereof.

British Library Cataloguing in Publication Data
A CIP catalogue record for this book
is available from the British Library

Empirical Methods for the Study of Labor Force Dynamics

ISBN13: 978-0-415-26940-7 (Hardback)
ISBN13: 978-0-415-86608-8 (Paperback)

EMPIRICAL METHODS FOR THE STUDY OF LABOR FORCE DYNAMICS

FUNDAMENTALS OF PURE AND APPLIED ECONOMICS

EDITORS IN CHIEF

J. LESOURNE, Conservatoire National des Arts et Métiers, Paris, France

H. SONNENSCHEIN, University of Pennsylvania, Philadelphia, PA, USA

ADVISORY BOARD

K. ARROW, Stanford, CA, USA
W. BAUMOL, Princeton, NJ, USA
W. A. LEWIS, Princeton, NJ, USA
S. TSURU, Tokyo, Japan

LABOUR ECONOMICS
In 2 Volumes

Empirical Methods for the Study of Labor Force Dynamics

Kenneth I. Wolpin

University of Pennsylvania, USA

A volume in the Labor Economics section

edited by

Finis Welch

Texas A&M University, Texas, USA

harwood academic publishers

Australia · Austria · China · France · Germany · India · Japan · Luxembourg · Malaysia
Netherlands · Russia · Singapore · Switzerland · Thailand · United Kingdom · United States.

3 Boulevard Royal
L-2449 Luxembourg

British Library Cataloguing in Publication Data

Wolpin, Kenneth I.
  Empirical Methods for the Study of Labor
  Force Dynamics. – (Fundamentals of
  Pure & Applied Economics Series,
  ISSN 0191-1708; Vol.60)
  I. Title II. Series
  331.11072

ISBN 3-7186-5738-4

Contents

Introduction to the Series

Drawing on a personal network, an economist can still relatively easily stay well informed in the narrow field in which he works, but to keep up with the development of economics as a whole is a much more formidable challenge. Economists are confronted with difficulties associated with the rapid development of their discipline. There is a risk of "balkanization" in economics, which may not be favorable to its development.

Fundamentals of Pure and Applied Economics has been created to meet this problem. The discipline of economics has been subdivided into sections (listed at the back of this volume). These sections comprise short books, each surveying the state of the art in a given area.

Each book starts with the basic elements and goes as far as the most advanced results. Each should be useful to professors needing material for lectures, to graduate students looking for a global view of a particular subject, to professional economists wishing to keep up with the development of their science, and to researchers seeking convenient information on questions that incidentally appear in their work.

Each book is thus a presentation of the state of the art in a particular field rather than a step-by-step analysis of the development of the literature. Each is a high-level presentation but accessible to anyone with a solid background in economics, whether engaged in business, government, international organizations, teaching, or research in related fields.

Three aspects of *Fundamentals of Pure and Applied Economics* should be emphasized:

- First, the project covers the whole field of economics, not only theoretical or mathematical economics.
- Second, the project is open-ended and the number of books is not predetermined. If new and interesting areas appear, they will generate additional books.
- Last, all the books making up each section will later be grouped to constitute one or several volumes of an Encyclopedia of Economics.

The editors of the sections are outstanding economists who have selected as authors for the series some of the finest specialists in the world.

Empirical Methods for the Study of Labor Force Dynamics

KENNETH I. WOLPIN

University of Pennsylvania, USA

1. INTRODUCTION

In the last twenty years there has been an explosion of economic research on labor force dynamics, the movement of individuals between labor force states. The recent book by Devine and Kiefer (1991) provides an annotated bibliography of over 100 studies and a reference list of over 500 studies. Indicative of the literature's maturity, there are now several excellent surveys which are either devoted to specific components of the literature or to providing a more general overview.[1]* There are also articles and books devoted to the statistical methodology for the analysis of transition data that use as a primary substantive focus the topic of labor force dynamics.[2]

This essay** focuses on the methods by which behavioral theories of labor force dynamics have been empirically implemented. Most attention is paid to the partial equilibrium two-state transition model of job search behavior. That model is the foundation for much of our thinking about the nature of unemployment at both the individual and aggregate levels. Since at least the early 1970s the simple sequential optimal stopping formulation of McCall (1970) and of Mortensen (1970) has served as the basis for interpreting data on unemployment spells and (accepted) wage distributions, and for studying policy interventions such as unemployment insurance programs. Although the basic formulation has remained the same, approaches to the empirical implementation of such models have changed dramatically.

Chapter 2 surveys a small set of empirical papers based on the two-state model in order to reveal the progression of thought about estimation methodology. Given this goal there is no attempt to provide a broad survey

---

* Numbered footnotes are located in the Notes section starting on page 73.

** Support from NSF grant SES-9109607 and from the C.V. Starr Center for Applied Economics, New York University, is gratefully acknowledged. The author has benefitted from discussions with Zvi Eckstein, Chris Flinn and Mike Keane.

of the empirical literature. In presenting such a selective review, the reader should be aware that the papers that have been chosen are in large part intended to be representative or illustrative of particular approaches. There is no intention, except where clearly stated, of assigning original contributions to particular authors. A further goal is to attempt to go beyond description and critique. Most of the literature has assumed that the theoretical job search framework is in fact an apt description of actual job search behavior at least as an 'as if' characterization. There has been little attention to the issue of testing this assumption. Exactly what would constitute a test of the two-state job search framework is not a simple matter. However, after 20 years of empirical research, it seems appropriate to explore the question of whether the framework is a suitable foundation for the analysis of unemployment data.

Section one of this chapter begins with a presentation of the standard two-state job search model. As noted, there have been several recent surveys of this literature (e.g. Mortensen, 1986) which provide considerable theoretical detail, so what is presented, while self-contained, is only what is sufficient background for the points that follow. Section two discusses the empirical implications of the theory and the next section presents facts about the distribution of unemployment duration and accepted wages from a number of data sources. The capability of the job search model to explain these facts is explored. The fourth section discusses attempts at empirical implementation, including early and later reduced form methods based on regression and hazard function approaches, the more recent structural approach, and the experimental approach. The final section of this chapter presents an equilibrium labor market search model that has recently been implemented.

The terms 'reduced form' and 'structural' estimation do not have universally accepted meanings. In this essay structural estimation refers to estimation that has as its intent recovery of the fundamental parameters of the theoretical optimization problem. Estimation methods that recover parameters that are (often unspecified) functions of the fundamental parameters, such as linear approximations of the decision functions not explicitly derived from the decision functions themselves, fall into the reduced form category. Empirical work that is conducted absent an explicit optimization problem is by definition reduced form. Comparisons between reduced form and structural estimation approaches in the job search context, because of the inherent simplicity of the model, will hopefully help to clarify the distinction.

The existence of a large body of empirical work devoted to understanding the single unemployment-to-employment transition, and in particular its systematic evolution and progress, distinguishes this empirical literature from any other area of research on labor force dynamics. Unlike the optimal stopping model of job search, there is no behavioral model of other labor force transitions which is so universally accepted as the basis for empirical work, nor is there any substantial body of empirical work on other labor force transitions. It is therefore not possible to provide as systematic a discussion of empirical methods that have been adopted for the study of other labor force transitions.

Rather than attempt what would be a disconnected review of that research, in keeping with the theme of this essay two further areas of research on labor force dynamics are addressed that are related to empirical methodology. Chapter 3 considers the question of whether there are distinct non-employment states. Not only is it a natural extension of the two-state model to allow for distinct unemployment and out-of-the labor force states, but the issue is of clear policy importance. Indeed, the relatively small amount of empirical effort devoted to the issue does not seem to be commensurate with its significance. In part, this paucity of attention my be due to a lack of sufficiently detailed event history data on search activities. The two-state model is nested in the three-state model in a way that permits tests of the distinction in both reduced form (semi-parametric) and structural formats. An estimable structural model which allows for reporting bias is presented and empirical findings in the literature are briefly discussed.

Chapter 4 discusses a question that has received considerable attention in the labor economics literature, that of distinguishing between alternative explanations of the observed wage-tenure relationship. In the first section, the simplest type of job turnover model, in which competing wage offers are received while employed, is presented and shown to imply a positive cross-sectional wage-tenure relationship. A human capital motivated wage offer function is then embedded in the model and the issue of separating out the alternative explanations with data is discussed. Again, it is the fact that the two models are nested in a more general formulation that facilitates relative attribution of the observed wage-tenure relationship to the 'alternatives'. In the following sections, two different approaches to the estimation of the wage-tenure relationship, Topel's (1991) two-step estimation procedure and Wolpin's (1992) structural turnover model, are presented in some detail.

The overall theme illustrated by these last two chapters is that many hypotheses concerned with labor force dynamic behavior can be embedded in general optimizing models and their relative contributions can be assessed in that context. It is more reasonable to suppose that the many alternative explanations of the small set of available facts about the patterns of labor force transitions co-reside than to suppose that one explanation is hegemonous to the exclusion of all others. With this in mind, Chapter 5 relates behavioral models of labor force dynamics to the recent literature on estimating discrete choice dynamic programming models more generally. The chapter reviews a number of methods that have been suggested in that literature for empirically implementing these models.

Chapter 6 provides some brief concluding remarks on directions for future research.

2. THE TWO-STATE JOB SEARCH MODEL

2.1 Theory

In this section, the discrete time two-state job search model is developed. Consider an infinitely-lived individual searching sequentially for a job over a finite horizon of length T. The finite horizon can be motivated by the existence of borrowing constraints. At the beginning of each period, $t = 1 \ldots T - 1$ the individual receives an offer of employment with probability p, having paid a search cost of c in the prior period. The individual begins the unemployment spell at $t = 0$, and at $t = 1$ the individual has been unemployed one period. The per-period wage associated with any particular job offer (wages are the only dimension of compensation) is drawn from a distribution function $F(w)$. Once a wage offer is accepted the per-period wage is fixed. In this setting, the parameters p and c, and the function F are fundamental to the individual, i.e. there is no more fundamental decision made by the agent determining them. Thus, for example, search intensity cannot be chosen to influence the probability of receiving an offer.

The individual's objective is to maximize expected wealth. One natural assumption to make about the decision process when the end of the search horizon is reached is that at that point the individual must accept the next offer that is received.[3] Adopting this assumption and also assuming that individuals remain on the same job forever, then given that the individual has not received and accepted an offer by the last period, i.e. at $T - 1$, expected wealth at the beginning of period T, denoted by V_T, is given by

$$V_T = p\frac{\mu}{1-\beta} + (1-p)[-c + \beta V_T]$$

$$= \frac{p\dfrac{\mu}{1-\beta} - c(1-p)}{1-(1-p)\beta}, \tag{1}$$

where μ is the mean of the wage offer distribution, and $\beta = 1/(1+r)$ is the discount factor, with r the market interest rate. With probability p the individual expects to receive the infinitely discounted wage $\mu/(1-\beta)$, while with probability $1 - p$ the individual must continue to search, paying c and receiving the same one period discounted value of expected wealth, βV_T.

Given the assumption that jobs last forever, lifetime wealth at time t for an individual with a current wage offer w that is accepted is

$$V_t^a(w) = \frac{w}{1-\beta}, \qquad t \le T-1, \tag{2}$$

while expected lifetime wealth given continued search is

$$V_t^s = -c + \beta\Big[pE\max\big(V_{t+1}^s, V_{t+1}^a(w)\big) + (1-p)V_{t+1}^s\Big], \qquad t \le T-2, \tag{3}$$

At $T-1$, $V_{T-1}^s = -c + \beta V_T$. In (3), the expectations operator, conditioned on the information set at t, is written under the assumption that no new information arrives between t and $t+1$. This assumption rules out, for example, serial correlation in wage draws.[4]

Letting w_t^*, the reservation wage, be the value of the wage at $t \le T-2$ that equates (2) and (3), it is straightforward to show that the reservation wage must satisfy the difference equation

$$\frac{w_t^*}{1-\beta} = -c + \frac{\beta}{1-\beta}w_{t+1}^* + \frac{\beta}{1-\beta}p\int_{w_{t+1}^\circ}^{\infty}\big(w - w_{t+1}^*\big)\,dF(w), \tag{4}$$

where (4) is obtained by using the fact that $w_t^* = V_t^s(1-\beta)$. At $t = T-1$, $w_{T-1}^* = (1-\beta)[-c + \beta V_T]$ while at T the reservation wage is by definition zero; any offer is accepted. It is clear from (1) through (3) that a unique positive reservation wage exists at each t as long as the cost of search is not too large, that is, as long as $V_t^s > 0$ for each t. The individual's decision rule is to accept an offer at t (assuming one is obtained) if and only if the wage offer at t exceeds the reservation wage at t, $w_t > w_t^*$; otherwise, the individual continues to search. The first-order difference equation for the reservation wage can be solved numerically by backwards recursion given specific numerical values for the fundamentals, including F.

The reservation wage in the infinite horizon problem is the limit of the time-dependent reservation wages as T tends to infinity and is found by setting $w_t^* = w_{t+1}^* = w^*$ in (4), namely[5]

$$w^* = -c + \frac{\beta}{1-\beta}\, p \int_{w^*}^{\infty} \left(w - w^*\right) dF(w).$$ (5)

The reservation wage equation, (4) or (5), contains all of the restrictions provided by the theory.[6] Reduced form approaches to estimation use 'approximations' to the reservation wage equation, while structural approaches attempt to embed the solution to the reservation wage equation explicitly in the estimation.

2.2 Empirical Implications

Empirical implications of economic models are often couched in terms of comparative static (dynamic) predictions, namely how decisions change with changes in exogenous components of the model. In the job search model, the decision rule of whether to accept or reject an offer once received depends on the reservation wage given by (4) or (5) while the exogenous factors are the cost of search, the offer probability, and the offer wage distribution parameters. It is useful in presenting the comparative static results to define the hazard rate at t, h_t. The hazard rate, the probability of leaving unemployment at t conditional on being unemployed up to time t, is

$$h_t = p \int_{w_t^*}^{\infty} dF(w),$$ (6)

the probability of receiving an offer at t times the probability of accepting the offer. In the infinite horizon model the hazard rate is constant, $h_t = h$. Notice that, in equation (5), the derivative of the object $p \int_{w^*}^{\infty} \left(w - w^*\right) dF(w)$ with respect to w^* is equal to the negative of the hazard rate. Given this fact, comparative static predictions are easily derived for the infinite horizon model, namely,

$$\frac{dw^*}{dc} = -\frac{r}{r+h} < 0,$$

$$\frac{dw^*}{dp} = \frac{r\left(w^* + c\right)}{p(r+h)} > 0,$$

$$\frac{dw^*}{d\beta} = \left(\frac{r}{1+r}\right)^2 \frac{w^* + c}{r+h} > 0,$$

$$\frac{dw^*}{d\mu} = \frac{h}{r+h} > 0. \tag{7}$$

The reservation wage varies inversely with the cost of search, and directly with the job offer probability, the discount factor, and the mean of the wage offer distribution. It is also possible to show that the reservation wage will increase as the spread of the wage distribution increases in a mean-preserving sense (see Mortensen, 1986). Similar predictions hold in the finite horizon case and are obtained by differentiating (4) recursively.[7] However, contrary to the constant value of search in the infinite horizon case, the existence of a terminal search date in the finite horizon case leads to a declining value of search as the horizon is approached. Thus, with the finite horizon, the reservation wage falls and the hazard rate rises with the duration of unemployment.[8]

Comparative static predictions have empirical content only if they are related to observables. Although we do not observe reservation wages directly, there exist some surveys which ask questions designed to elicit responses that correspond to the notion of a reservation wage. For example, in each annual survey of the 1979 youth cohort of the National Longitudinal Surveys of Labor Market Experience, respondents who are unemployed at the time of the survey are asked the question, 'What would the wage or salary have to be for you to be willing to take a job?' The issue most often raised about using such data is that it is not factual, but subjective. Economists tend to have a bias against using data that is not based on what individuals actually do. Thus, the argument would be that finding responses that do not correspond to the model's comparative static predictions could be due to the respondents either interpreting the question differently than was intended or the respondent not taking the question seriously enough to provide a thoughtful response. Presumably, one could not find comfort if the responses did not violate comparative static predictions either. The argument, however, seems overstated. If the notion of a reservation wage strategy is at all descriptive of actual behavior, there should be no reason why current job seekers should be unable to accurately answer the survey question. Below we explore possible uses of reservation wage data.

Although reservation wage data may or may not be problematical, such information is more usually simply not available. However, the behavioral outcomes that result from optimal search, namely the duration of unemployment and the accepted wage, are observed in many data sets. Comparative static results with respect to statistics related to these observables, e.g. hazard rates and mean accepted wages, and analogous to (7), can also be derived although not all of them are signed.[9]

However, while these outcomes are often measured, the exogenous constraints are generally not. In most data sets individuals are not asked about the actual costs they have incurred while searching, nor about rejected offers, and in no widely used data set have individuals been asked about their perceived probability of receiving job offers or about the distribution of wage offers they believe themselves to face.[10] Thus, it is not possible to estimate directly the influence of the search environment on unemployment search outcomes nor to test the comparative static predictions of job search theory that arise from the assumption solely of optimization. Before turning to a discussion of the evolution of empirical methodology and questions about the testability of job search theory, consider first some of the facts about the unemployment to employment transition and the ways in which those facts can be explained by the job search model.

2.3 Some Facts

One way to summarize unemployment duration data is by tabulating the empirical counterpart of the hazard function (6), that is, the proportion of individuals unemployed at the beginning of each period who leave unemployment during that period. Such a calculation would be straightforward if all individuals were observed to have completed their spells of unemployment. However, incomplete spells often arise in the collection of unemployment data. The Kaplan–Meier non-parametric estimator of the hazard function accounts for incomplete spells. It is formed by dividing the number of exits during a period by the number who could have survived to the beginning of the next period (were observed to either exit or not exit during the period). It can be interpreted as the maximum likelihood estimator of the hazard function (see Kalbfleisch and Prentice, 1980).

Table 1 presents the Kaplan–Meier hazard function for three different data sets. The first two are based on administrative records of unemployment compensation beneficiaries, one from Canada (Ham and Rea, 1987) and the other from twelve states in the U.S. (Meyer, 1990). The third is based on data from a U.S. longitudinal survey, the 1979 youth cohort of the National Longitudinal Surveys of Labor Market Experience sponsored by the U.S. Bureau of Labor Statistics (Eckstein and Wolpin, 1992). The data based on the administrative records depicts the duration in weeks to re-employment for Canadian males between 1975 and 1980 and for U.S. males between 1978 and 1983, while the NLSY data depicts the duration in

TABLE 1

Kaplan–Meier Hazard Function Estimates: Duration and Unemployment

	Canadian Administrative Records[a] (weeks)	U.S. Administrative Records[b] (weeks)	NLSY[c] (quarters)
0	—	—	.468
1	.171	.082	.137
2	.170	.066	.074
3	.098	.056	.072
4	.066	.061	.040
5	.062	.050	.043
6	.076	.049	.013
7	.051	.042	.026
8	.068	.041	.020
9	.041	.046	.010
10	.064	.037	.016
11	.038	.042	.015
12	.048	.060	.010
13	.059	.061	.013
14	.048	.045	.003
15	.026	.041	.003
16	.054	.056	.010
17	.054	.058	
18	.043	.047	
19	.017	.047	
20	.065	.059	
21	.039	.058	
22	.056	.061	
23	.040	.051	
24	.026	.079	
25	.009	.105	

[a] Ham and Rea (1987).
[b] Meyer (1990).
[c] Eckstein and Wolpin (1992): White Male High School Graduates.

quarters between permanently leaving high school and obtaining the first full-time job for a nationally representative sample of white males who graduated from high school between 1978 and 1984.[11] The most obvious characteristic of all three hazard functions is the initial decline in the hazard followed by a period of relative constancy. In the case of the administrative data, truncating duration at 25 weeks hides some of the increase in hazard rates that occurs later (see page 26).

A second important feature of the data that is, unfortunately, rarely reported is the relationship of accepted wages to duration. Neither the Ham and Reas nor the Meyer data provides information on accepted wages. For the NLSY data used by Eckstein and Wolpin, the regression coefficient of duration in an accepted wage regression with no other regressors is negative and statistically significant at the .01 level. The magnitude is fairly small, with each additional quarter of search associated with a lower mean accepted quarterly wage of 54 dollars (about 2 percent of the mean wage). Although it is unclear whether this is a general result, it is useful for the sake of argument to assume that it is.[12] It should be understood that this relationship is not to be interpreted as the effect on accepted wages of exogenously altering the duration of unemployment; accepted wages and unemployment duration are determined jointly (see below).

Consider the question of whether either the finite or infinite horizon model can generate these facts without additional assumptions. Consider the case of a homogenous population. The infinite horizon model predicts a constant, and equal, hazard rate for each individual in the population because reservation wages are constant and equal. Any sample drawn from a population in which each individual has the same constant hazard function would tend to exhibit a constant hazard rate, that is, the proportion of individuals exiting unemployment in each period would tend not to change with the duration of unemployment and would tend to be equal to the constant hazard faced by each individual. Further, with a constant and equal reservation wage, the mean accepted wage will also not vary with the duration of unemployment. The finite horizon model, on the other hand, predicts that each individual will have an increasing hazard rate because reservation wages optimally decline. Mean accepted wages will decline with duration, as in the NLSY data, because reservation wages decline. Under the homogeneity assumption, any sample will tend to have the same characteristics. Thus, with a homogenous population, neither of the two models can explain the crude facts.

There are two possible modifications of the above argument that seem reasonable to pursue, admitting to population (and sample) heterogeneity in some fundamentals and/or allowing for additional forms of non-stationarity. Consider first the infinite horizon model and suppose, for example, that within the population (and sample), individuals differ in their cost of search, c. Those with high values of c will have low reservation wages, while those with low values of c will have high reservation wages. However, while an individual's reservation wage does not vary with duration, and thus, each individual's hazard rate is also constant, the population hazard rate will be declining. The first individuals to accept offers will be those with lower reservation wages and so as time proceeds the sample of searchers will become disproportionately composed of high reservation (low c) types. As demonstrated by the preceding intuition, and as is well known, unobserved heterogeneity will induce negative duration dependence, i.e. declining hazard rates. But, the other implication of this form of heterogeneity is that mean accepted wages will increase with duration, which is inconsistent with the facts. In order to explain both facts, it is necessary that the high reservation wage types accept lower offers on average. This can occur only if those individuals with low costs of search, in the example, also face wage offer distributions with low means, while still preserving high reservation wages.

Consider next the finite horizon model and suppose that, for example, additional duration dependence arises because the probability of receiving an offer declines with the duration of unemployment in a way that is known to individuals at the beginning of their unemployment spell.While this will cause the reservation wage to decline even faster, the hazard rate, which is the product of the offer probability and the acceptance rate, may now decline rather than rise with duration. Thus, as with the infinite horizon model, the facts can be explained with additional assumptions. Of course, the finite horizon model can include unobserved heterogeneity in fundamental parameters as well, inducing a variety of patterns for hazard rates and accepted wages.

2.4 Estimation

2.4.1 Reduced Form Approaches

a. Regression models.

Most early studies used a regression framework loosely motivated by the two-state job search model presented above. Many of these studies had as a main concern estimating the effect of unemployment compensation benefits on the duration of unemployment. Unemployment compensation is a subsidy to search and should have the effect of increasing the reservation wage as in (6), reducing the hazard rate in each period that benefits are available, and therefore increasing the average duration of unemployment.[13] This specific modification of the search model is considered when structural estimation approaches are discussed and provides a concrete point of comparison between alternative reduced form methods and between reduced form and structural methods. Because of this strong comparative static prediction, estimating the effect of unemployment compensation on unemployment duration provides a test of the basic job search model as well as being of direct policy interest. It is the one example in the literature of a directly estimable counterpart to a comparative static prediction.

To motivate reduced form regression methods that were prominent in the early literature, assume that available data consist of completed unemployment spells together with accepted wage offers for a random sample of individuals. Letting f_d be the discrete probability of unemployment duration d, that is, the probability of receiving and rejecting an offer or not receiving an and offer through $t = d - 1$ and receiving and accepting and offer at time $t = d$, expected duration of unemployment, $\sum df_d$, in the finite horizon case is given by

$$
\begin{aligned}
E(d) &= \sum_{d=1}^{\infty} d(1 - h_0)(1 - h_1) \dots (1 - h_{d-1}) h_d \\
&= \sum_{d=1}^{T-1} d(1 - h_0)(1 - h_1) \dots (1 - h_{d-1})(h_d) \\
&\quad + \left[(1 - h_0) \dots (1 - h_{T-1}) \right] \left(T + \frac{1-p}{p} \right).
\end{aligned} \tag{8}
$$

where $h_0 = 0$. With constant offer probabilities, hazard rates are increasing with duration $t = T$ (recall that reservation wages decline with duration) and then are constant and equal to p as a consequence of the assumption that reservation wages are zero after $T - 1$. In the infinite horizon case expected duration is the inverse of the constant hazard rate.[14] The hazard rates in (8) are given by (6). Thus, expected duration is a function of the offer probability, of the parameters of the wage offer distribution function, and of either the stationary reservation wage in the infinite horizon case or the entire set of duration-dated reservation wages through $t = d$ in the finite horizon case. Any transformation of duration, such as log duration, will be different function of the same factors.[15]

The accepted wage distribution function at t is $F(w)/(1 - F(w_t^*))$. The expected accepted wage at t is given by

$$E\left(w_t | w_t > w_t^*\right) = \int_{w_t^o}^{\infty} \frac{w}{1 - F\left(w_t^*\right)} \, dF(w) \tag{9}$$

and is thus a function of the reservation wage at t and of F. In the infinite horizon case w^* replaces w_t^* in (9).

A linear approximation to a regression equation system for equations (4), (8) and (9) would be

$$d = \alpha_0 + \alpha_1 p + \alpha_2 \mu + \sum_{t=1}^{T} \alpha_{3t} w_t^* + u_1,$$

$$w_t^a = \gamma_0 + \gamma_1 \mu + \gamma_2 w_t^* + u_2,$$

$$w_t^* = \beta_0 + \beta_1 c + \beta_2 p + \beta_3 \mu + \beta_4 r + \beta_5 (T - t) \tag{10}$$

where w_t^a and w_t^* represent the accepted wage and reservation wage after t periods of unemployment and where, for convenience, μ, the mean of F, is the only parameter of the wage offer distribution that is assumed to vary in the population. Note that the reservation wage at t depends on the number of periods remaining until the end of the horizon $T - t$ rather than on t. Regardless of the length of the horizon, the reservation wage will be the same at all times equidistant from the date of the finite horizon. The regression equation for the offered wage is $w^o = \mu +$ error. Note that the duration and accepted wage equation errors (u_1 and u_2) represent deviations from conditional means, while except for approximation error associated with its linearization, the reservation wage equation is exactly represented. Of course, estimation error could arise in w_t^* if reservation wages were reported with error.

The earlier regression-based studies did not attempt to recover the 'structural' parameters in (10), but rather the parameters of the reduced form of (10), namely

$$d = \pi_{01} + \pi_{11} p + \pi_{21} \mu + \pi_{31} c + \pi_{41} T + \pi_{51} r + v_1,$$

$$w_t^a = \pi_{02} + \pi_{12} p + \pi_{22} \mu + \pi_{32} c + \pi_{42} T + \pi_{52} r + v_2,$$

$$w_t^* = \pi_{03} + \pi_{13} p + \pi_{23} \mu + \pi_{33} c + \pi_{43} T + \pi_{53} r + v_3. \tag{11}$$

Unfortunately, as noted, very few data sets provide direct measures of any of the regressors in (11). The resolution has been to assume that these regressors are related to observable variables.

The paper by Ehrenberg and Oaxaca (1976) provides a useful example of these pioneering studies.[16] In Ehrenberg and Oaxaca's formulation of the reduced form, the log of unemployment duration and the log of the accepted wage are used as the dependent variables.[17] Their motivation is to estimate the responsiveness of unemployment duration (d) and the accepted wage (w^a) to the unemployment benefit replacement ratio, measured as the fraction of the individual's pre-unemployment wage that is replaced by the insurance. As noted, viewed as a reduction in the cost of search, an increase in the replacement ratio should increase the reservation wage, thereby increasing the duration of search and the post-unemployment or accepted wage.

Because so much of the literature is concerned with this policy question, it is useful to understand the motivation for the use of the replacement ratio in this reduced form, that is, the division of benefits by the pre-unemployment wage, as opposed to benefits alone. Although not all studies have continued to use the replacement ratio as the appropriate measure for estimating the impact of unemployment insurance programs, the use of the pre-unemployment wage as a regressor is practically universal.[18]

The first point to note is that the reduced form for duration given by (11) does not include the pre-unemployment wage. If one has complete information about the cost of search, the probability of receiving job offers, the parameters of the wage offer distribution, the search horizon, and the discount rate, then the pre-unemployment wage should be irrelevant to the determination of the duration of an unemployment spell. Lacking direct measures of these variables, researchers have used the pre-unemployment wage as a proxy.[19] The specific variable which the pre-unemployment wage has been assumed to proxy is most usually the mean of the wage offer distribution, the permanent component of wages being related to unmeasured skills. If the generosity of unemployment insurance programs varies geographically in a way that is related to the level of wages in the area, then benefit effects on duration estimated from such geographic variation excluding the proxy will be confounded with the effect of differences in wage offer distributions on duration.

A second reason for including the pre-unemployment wage is that unemployment compensation benefits are usually tied to it at least up to some level. Higher benefits, for a given unemployment insurance scheme, may therefore capture in part the effect of individuals with higher pre-unemployment wages having faced higher mean wage offer distributions (Welch, 1977). By itself the higher mean leads to a shorter unemployment spell; a one dollar increase in the mean of the wage offer distribution increases the reservation wage by less than one dollar (see equation (7)). Thus, excluding the pre-unemployment wage would bias the estimated benefit effect on duration if individuals differ in their wage offer distributions in ways that cannot be measured.

Although omitted variable bias seems to be well understood, the potential for bias introduced by using proxy variables is less well appreciated. To understand the source of the problem, what I will refer to as proxy variable bias, note that the pre-unemployment wage must have been itself the outcome of a prior search unemployment spell. To make the case most strongly, assume that the duration of the prior spell was governed by exactly the same behavioral process and constraints as the current spell. Such an assumption is consistent with a model in which there are exogenous layoffs so that unemployment spells are renewal processes. In particular, assume that the replacement ratio is identical in the two spells, as would be the case if each individual resided in the same geographic area during each spell and there were no changes in the parameters of the UI program. Now, the problem with using the prior wage as a proxy for the mean of the wage offer distribution is that, as seen in (11), the prior wage is a function of all of the determinants of duration, not just the mean of the wage offer distribution.

To simplify the discussion, write duration as a function only of the benefit level and the mean of the wage offer distribution, namely

$$d = \pi_1 B + \pi_2 \mu + \epsilon, \qquad (12)$$

where the π coefficients signify that (12) is a reduced form as in (11). Now μ is unobserved and omitting it leads to the usual bias, which can be written as

$$E\left(\hat{\pi}_1 - \pi_1\right) = \frac{\sigma^2_{\pi_2\mu}}{\sigma^2_B} \, \beta_{B,\pi_2\mu} \qquad (13)$$

where $\hat{\pi}_1$ is the ols estimate of π_1, and $\beta_{B,\pi_2\mu}$ is the regression coefficient obtained from a regression of B on $\pi_2 \mu$. Benefits and the wage offer mean may be correlated for either of the reasons given above.

Now, the pre-unemployment wage (w^a_{-1}), itself determined in part by μ as the outcome of a prior search, can be written as

$$w_{-1}^a = \pi_3 \mu + \omega. \tag{14}$$

The 'measurement error' in (14), ω, contains in it all of the other determinants of w_{-1}^a in (11). In this example that set consists only of B, so ω and B must be correlated. Solving (14) for μ and substituting into (12) yields a regression equation of the form

$$d = \pi_1 B + \frac{\pi_2}{\pi_3} w_{-1}^a - \frac{\pi_2}{\pi_3} \omega + \epsilon. \tag{15}$$

The bias in the ols estimate of π_1, in this case, can be shown to be

$$E(\hat{\pi}_1 - \pi_1) = \frac{\sigma_\omega^2 \, \sigma_{\pi_2\mu}^2}{\sigma_B^2 \, \sigma_{w_{-1}^a}^2 - \left(\sigma_{B,w_{-1}^a}\right)^2} \left(\beta_{B,\pi_2\mu} - \pi_3\beta_{B,\omega}\right) \tag{16}$$

where the $\beta's$ again refer to regression coefficients with the first subscript referring to the dependent variable.

If B an ω are uncorrelated, then the bias in the estimate of π_1 results from the measurement error introduced by the proxy variable. The bias is always reduced by including the proxy; in terms of bias, estimating (15) is always better than estimating (14).[20] However, if B and ω are correlated, as theory suggests, then the choice of estimator is ambiguous. The bias when the proxy is included can be smaller or larger in absolute value and can even be of a different sign than that of the omitted variable bias. The implicit assumption made by essentially all researchers who have estimated the effect of unemployment compensation on duration is that omitted variable bias is a more serious problem than proxy variable bias. As shown above, however, the value of proxies in bias reduction cannot be ascertained without reference to the theory. Indeed, it is ironic that if the individuals in the sample do not differ in wage offer distributions they face, or if the differences can be well measured by observable characteristics, then the variation in benefits induced by its relation to the prior wage is exactly of the right kind. Under the assumptions of the search model variation in the prior wage around the mean of the wage offer distribution is purely random.

Proxy variables tend to proliferate in many empirical applications of job search theory. For example, variables used in the Ehrenberg–Oaxaca reduced form regressions, in addition to the replacement ratio and the (log) pre-unemployment wage, include the following regressors: race, marital status, home ownership, number of dependents, expected number of years to retirement, the local area unemployment rate, the size of the local area population, net family assets, non-labor income, job tenure with prior employer, age, health status, education, and several others that are specific to the age-sex composition of the sample. Not all of these variables are proxies in the sense of the pre-unemployment wage. Race, or age, for example, are not determined by μ, but are possibly determinants of μ (or c, or p in the more complete search model context). While including relevant exogenous variables, such as race or age, is usually helpful in interpretation, most of the variables in the above list are not easily categorized. Some of them may be determined by μ (viewed generally as earnings opportunities) but be uncorrelated with B, given μ. Others may be like the pre-unemployment wage proxy and still others may be exogenous. As much thought needs to be given to what variables are to be included in empirical analyses as is given to what variables may have been omitted, particularly when potentially included variables are not explicitly treated in the theory.

It is well known that it is possible to get something that looks like (10) and (11) in the infinite horizon case by assuming that the wage offer distribution is Pareto: $dF(w) = \phi w^\alpha \, dw$, where $\phi = -(\alpha + 1)/\gamma^{\alpha + 1}$, $\alpha \leq -2$ and $\gamma \leq w \leq \infty$. Then, it is easy to show that

$$E\left(\ln w \mid w \geq w^*\right) = -\ln \gamma + \mu_{\ln w} + \ln w^*, \tag{17}$$

where $\mu_{\ln w}$ is the mean of $\ln w$, which leads to a regression specification for accepted wages that is identical to (10) with the variables measured in $\ln$'s. In addition, with a constant hazard the expected value of the $\ln$ of duration is given by

$$E \ln d = \alpha_0 - \ln p + (\alpha + 1)\mu_{\ln w} - (\alpha + 1)\ln w^*. \tag{18}$$

Equation (18) is identical to (10) with the variables in $\ln$s. Now, it is clear that there is very little in (17) and (18) that results from the assumptions of the job search model except for the existence of a reservation wage policy. Substituting a $\ln$ version of the reservation wage equation shown in (10) into (17) and (18) yields a form like (11). Notice, however, that if one is willing to make assumptions about the relationship between specific exogenous observables and specific fundamental parameters, there can be seen to be testable cross-equation restrictions in the analog to (11) in the Pareto case.[21] For example, all variables that affect the cost of search but neither the mean of the (ln) wage offer distribution nor the probability of receiving an offer

must affect the accepted (ln) wage and (ln) duration in the same proportion.[22] But, such tests tell us very little about the validity of the job search
model because it is the determination of the reservation wage as given by (4)
or (5) that is at the root of the theory and the linear (or log-linear) approximation to the reservation wage in (11) embeds very little about that
determination in it.

It was assumed in the previous discussion that reservation wages were not
directly measured. Most of the early uses of reservation wage data
focused on testing the hypothesis that reservation wages decline with
duration, $\beta_5 > 0$ in (10).[23] The problem with estimating such a regression is
obvious from (10).[24] Unless we measure all of the other determinants of the
reservation wage, or the sample is homogenous (except for measurement
error), ols estimates of the reservation wage relation will be biased and
inconsistent because the duration of unemployment itself depends on the
duration-dependent reservation wage. And, the sign of the bias depends on
which elements of the complete specification are missing, costs of search,
offer probabilities, wage offer distribution parameters or the discount factor.
Furthermore, there exist no instruments for duration; there are no variables
that are correlated with duration that are not also correlated with the
reservation wage. This includes past and future reservation wages, even if
they are measured, which must be correlated with the current reservation
wage as is clear from the difference equation for reservation wages given by
(4). Thus, in this linear setup, the reservation wage parameters of (10) are
not estimable even when reservation wage data exist.

Lancaster (1985) provides examples of (ln) linear simultaneous
equations systems where reservation wages decline with duration as is
consistent with the finite horizon search model. Suppose one has cross-
sectional observations on reservation wages and elapsed durations. Then,
starting with a Pareto wage distribution and assuming that the reservation
wage falls with duration in an *ad hoc* parametric fashion until it reaches the
lower truncation point of the Pareto distribution, at which point it is constant
at that lowest wage offer, Lancaster derives a linear equation relating the ln
of duration to the current reservation wage. Although, as noted above, the
ad hoc reservation wage function is not estimable by using exclusionary
restrictions, as there are in principle none, the (ln) duration equation is
estimable if there exist measured variables which affect the reservation
wage but not duration conditional on the reservation wage. This amounts to
the assumption that there are observable variables that are correlated with

the cost of search, but not the probability of receiving an offer nor the wage offer distribution. Lancaster and Chesher (1983) assume that the number of dependent children satisfies that restriction, affecting unemployment compensation benefit levels as it does in the English case. Whether that is a valid restriction is open to debate; fertility is not uncorrelated with income.

Kiefer and Neumann (1979) was possibly the first study to use restrictions from the theory to recover parameters of the reservation wage function. However, because they maintain the linear approximation for the reservation wage as in (10), their study is classified as a reduced form. But, rather than specifying duration and accepted wage regressions, they use a maximum likelihood approach based on the observation that acceptances and rejections are determined by a comparison between the offered wage and the reservation wage. With additional assumptions discussed below, they are able to identify the parameters of the (linearized) reservation wage function without the use of reservation wage data. However, their main focus was not on recovering the duration dependence parameter in the reservation wage function; their model is formally specified in the infinite horizon context.

Kiefer and Neumann assume a reservation wage equation of the form

$$w^* = X_c \beta_c + X_{cw} \beta_{cw} + X_w \beta_w + \epsilon_1, \tag{19}$$

where X_c are variables that affect only the cost of search, X_{cw} are variables that affect both the cost of search and the mean of the wage offer distribution, and X_w are variables that affect only the wage offer mean. In the finite horizon analogue, duration is explicitly entered as regressor. They consider only the case where job searchers receive one offer each period with certainty ($p = 1$). The discount factor is assumed to be constant in the sample. The error term in (19), which arises from incomplete data on the determinants of the reservation wage, is assumed to be normal with mean zero and constant variance (constant with respect to the X's and with respect to the duration of unemployment), and as is customary, is assumed to be orthogonal to the included variables. The wage offer function is written as

$$w = X_{cw} \gamma_{cw} + X_w \gamma_w + \epsilon_2 \tag{20}$$

where the error is also assumed to be normal with zero mean and constant variance, and is orthogonal to the included variables. The reservation wage error and the wage offer error are allowed to be correlated.

The hazard rate in this case, $Pr\,(w > w^*)$, is given by

$$
1 - \Phi\left(\frac{X_{cw}}{\sigma}\left[\gamma_{cw}\left(1 - \frac{\partial w^*}{\partial \mu}\right) - \frac{\partial w^*}{\partial c}\frac{\partial c}{\partial X_{cw}}\right]\right.
$$

$$
\left. + \frac{X_w}{\sigma}\left[\gamma_w\left(1 - \frac{\partial w^*}{\partial \mu}\right)\right] + \frac{X_c}{\sigma}\left[-\frac{\partial w^*}{\partial c}\frac{\partial c}{\partial X_c}\right]\right) \qquad (21)
$$

where Φ is the standard cumulative normal, σ is the standard deviation of the difference $\epsilon_2 - \epsilon_1$, the multipliers of the X's in the cumulative expression represent the difference between the mean wage offer and the mean reservation wage, and the β's have been written as $\beta_c = -\dfrac{\partial w^*}{\partial c}\dfrac{\partial c}{\partial X_c}$, $\beta_w = \gamma_w\dfrac{\partial w^*}{\partial \mu}$, and $\beta_{cw} = \gamma_{cw}\dfrac{\partial w^*}{\partial \mu} + \dfrac{\partial w^*}{\partial c}\dfrac{\partial c}{\partial X_{cw}}$. Given (21), it is straightforward to specify the joint likelihood of duration and the observed wage and to estimate the parameters by maximum likelihood.

Identification issues can be addressed with reference to (21). First, as others have noted, the wage offer function is estimable as in a standard parametric selectivity correction problem. A first-stage 'reduced form' likelihood function for observed durations based on (21) can be used to form the Mills' ratio. As long as X_c is non-empty, identification of the wage offer function does not rely solely on the normal distribution assumption. Given the parameters of the wage offer function, the γ's in (20), the critical exclusion restriction for identification of the rest of the parameters is that there be variables that affect the wage offer mean that do not affect the cost of search, that X_w be non-empty. This enables the identification of $\left(1 - \dfrac{\partial w^*}{\partial \mu}\right)\Big/\sigma$ as seen in (21). To get further, Kiefer and Neumann note that in the infinite horizon model $\dfrac{\partial w^*}{\partial \mu}$ is given by $\dfrac{h/r}{1 + h/r}$ so that with knowledge of r and the reduced form estimate of h, $\dfrac{\partial w^*}{\partial \mu}$ and σ are separately identified. Given these, the reservation wage parameters, the β's, are estimable.[25] What Kiefer and Neumann showed, then, is that with a linearized reservation wage function, normal errors, a unitary offer probability, a known discount factor, and exclusionary restrictions, it is possible to recover the parameters of the reservation wage function and the wage offer function in an infinite horizon setting with information only on accepted wages and completed durations of unemployment.

Probably the most important issue with respect to the credibility of the estimates obtained using this methodology is the validity of the exclusionary restrictions. Recall, that what is required for identification is that there exist some variables that are related to the wage offer mean that are unrelated to the cost of search. For that role Kiefer and Neumann chose the wage on the previous job and tenure on the previous job. However, as with Ehrenberg and Oaxaca, because the prior wage can be viewed as the outcome of a previous search and thus correlated with all of the elements of the job search model that determine accepted wages, including the cost of search, it cannot satisfy the exclusionary restriction that was imposed. Similarly, the wage-tenure locus of the prior job, as well, will be related to the parameters of the prior search. Thus, unless prior job searches conform to a different behavioral model or the current search parameters are unrelated to those in past searches, it is not valid to use the outcomes of prior searches as the basis for the exclusionary restrictions needed for identification in this framework.

b. Hazard models

The hazard function for the discrete time finite horizon search model as given by (6) represents the probability of leaving unemployment at t given that the individual is still unemployed at the beginning of t. The survivor function at t is the probability of remaining unemployed up to t, i.e. not exiting prior to t, and so is given by $\prod_{\tau=1}^{t}(1 - h_\tau)$. The probability of having a duration of unemployment of exactly $t = d$ periods, the density function for d periods of unemployment, is the product of the survivor function at $t = d - 1$ and the hazard rate at $t = d$. The density function was already used in calculating the expected duration of unemployment (8).

An alternative reduced form approach to estimation of the search model is to choose a specific form for the hazard function. Indeed, over the last decade or so, the bulk of reduced form estimation has been conducted in this manner. The parameterization of the hazard function, as opposed to the density or survivor functions, is more common because many hypotheses are more naturally couched in terms of the dependence of exit rates on duration and observables.

Most applications of hazard model estimation have assumed a continuous, rather than a discrete, time setting. In continuous time, the hazard function represents the instantaneous rate of exit at some time t conditional on not having exited up to that time. As in the discrete time case it is equal to the ratio of the density to the survivor function. The three are related as follows:

$$S(t) = \exp\left(-\int_0^t h(u)\, du\right)$$

$$f(t) = h(t)S(t), \tag{22}$$

where $S(t)$ is the survivor function at t.[26] The hazard function is not a probability density function. It, however, is non-negative and must satisfy, in the non-degenerate case, the condition that $\int_0^\infty h(u)\, du = \infty$.[27]

There are conceptually compelling reasons to prefer the continuous time formulation. The primary reason is simply that it is more general and in that sense less arbitrary. Adopting a discrete time formulation requires that one decide on the unit of time that is relevant to the decision process being studied. Is the appropriate decision period for the job search model a day, a week, or a month? And, surely, it would be quite fortunate if duration data always corresponded to the correct decision period. On the other hand, not all instants in time are the same. The continuous time model that pertains to job search behavior on weekdays is not likely to be the same as that on weekends. The job offer rate, for example, is often assumed to come from a Poisson process with a time invariant parameter, when that is very unlikely to be correct. Of course, modeling the process incorrectly is not an argument against using the appropriate statistical framework. One should nevertheless recall that the hazard 'model' is itself only an approximation to the behavioral model, and the relevant question should be whether the assumption about the time unit is important in terms of the inferences that are drawn about behavior. To my knowledge, there has been no work on assessing the relative importance of this issue in the broader context of using approximations to the outcomes of a well specified decision model.

There are a number of reasons why hazard models have come to dominate the regression approach, primarily stemming from the inherent limitations of regression models when applied to duration data. There are two main problems that have been stressed in the literature. The first has to do with the characteristics of samples often used in studies that employ duration data and the second to the type of explanatory variables that are used.

It is often the case that duration spells are incomplete. Suppose, for example, that in a particular sample unemployment spells are truncated by the design of the survey to be at most D periods. For such a sample the expected (average) duration is not given by (8) and the linear regression approximation to (8) given by (10) or (11) would then be interpreted as an approximation to the sample's expected duration function. The partial derivatives associated with this duration function, and thus the estimated parameters of (10) or (11), would depend on D. Similarly, if the researcher restricted attention only to completed spells, as for example in Ehrenberg and Oaxaca, the expected duration of that sample would also depend on D, although in a different way than for the sample that included incomplete spells. Thus, as in all sample selection problems, the interpretation of the regression parameters depends on the sample selection rule.

In deriving (10) and (11) from the underlying search structure, it was assumed that the only source of non-stationarity arose from the finiteness of the search horizon. However, non-stationarity might arise because some of the fundamental parameters, such as search costs or offer probabilities, themselves vary with duration. With parameters that change with duration, the expected duration of unemployment would depend on the entire path of those parameters. Using observable proxies that also vary with duration is at best cumbersome in a regression context. And, using some set of summary statistics, e.g. the mean or the value of the variable at the beginning of the spell, does some violence to the spirit of the reduced form approximation. On the other hand, in the hazard approach, such duration-varying variables cause no special conceptual problems because the current hazard rate, as opposed to the expected duration, depends only on the relevant part of the current information set, that is, on the state space of the decision problem. Note that the state space may include lagged continuous duration-varying variables.[28]

The choice of the hazard function specification is akin to the choice of the functional form of a regression. A convenient, and frequently pursued, strategy is to choose a proportional hazard specification which factors the hazard into one component that depends on duration and another that depends on explanatory variables. The duration component is called the baseline hazard which is shifted up or down in a parallel fashion according to the values of the explanatory (possibly time-varying) variables. Either a functional form for the baseline hazard is chosen, the baseline hazard is estimated non-parametrically, or the baseline hazard is treated as a nuisance function that is partialed out in estimation. These methods have been treated extensively elsewhere. Given the theme of this essay, it is not important to provide specifics, nor is that necessary for the reader to be able to understand what follows.

Meyer (1990) provides an interesting example of the hazard approach to estimating the reduced form of the job search model. Meyer's primary objective is to study the role of the level and length of unemployment insurance benefits. The existence of a fixed length of eligibility for unemployment insurance has been explicitly incorporated into job search models (see Mortensen, 1977). The properties of that model are not very different from the finite horizon job search model presented above, but formal discussion is delayed until structural estimation is considered. Suffice it to say that the implication that reservation wages fall with the duration of unemployment is unchanged.

Formally, Meyer assumes a proportional hazard of the form

$$h_i(d) = h_0(d) \exp\left\{z_i(d)'\pi\right\} \tag{23}$$

where h_0 is the baseline hazard, $z_i(d)$ is a vector of duration-dependent variables for individual i, and π is a vector of reduced form parameters. To develop the estimation method, let D_i be the duration of unemployment for individual i and following Meyer write

$$Pr\left(D_i \geq d+1 \mid D_i \geq d\right) = \frac{S(d+1)}{S(d)}$$

$$= \exp\left[-\exp\left(z_i(d)'\pi + \gamma(d)\right)\right] \tag{24}$$

where it is assumed that $z_i(d)$ does not change between d and $d+1$ and where $\gamma(d) = \ln \int\limits_{d}^{d+1} h_0(u)\,du$. Then, the probability of observing a complete spell of length k_i is

$$Pr\left(D_i = k_i\right) = \left\{1 - \exp\left[-\exp\left(z_i(k_i)'\pi + \gamma(k_i)\right)\right]\right\}$$

$$x \prod_{d=0}^{k_i-1} \exp\left[-\exp\left(z_i(d)'\pi + \gamma(d)\right)\right] \tag{25}$$

and the probability of observing an incomplete spell is

$$Pr\left(D_i \geq k_i\right) = \prod_{d=0}^{k_i-1} \exp\left[-\exp\left(z_i(d)'\pi + \gamma(d)\right)\right] \qquad (26)$$

The sample likelihood is the appropriate sample product of (25) and (26). The parameters that are estimated are the π's and the $\gamma(k)$'s for $k = 1...K$ where K is some arbitrarily censored spell length. Notice that although (25) and (26) correspond to the probabilities associated with a discrete hazard model, they are obtained consistently from an underlying continuous time process. A parametric assumption about the baseline hazard would essentially restrict the pattern of the γ's.

Meyer uses date from Continuous Wage and Benefit History (CWBH) UI administrative records from twelve states for males who collected unemployment insurance during the 1978–1983 period. The interesting feature of this data is that the exact length of the eligibility period is reported for each individual in the sample and that it varies considerably. The Kaplan–Meier hazard function, based on this data, was reported in Table 1 for the first 25 weeks. Table 2 extends the data past 25 weeks and adds a second column (column 3) tabulating, as does Meyer, hazard rates by the number of weeks left until benefit exhaustion. As column 2 shows, the hazard rate declines with duration for the first 9–10 weeks of unemployment and then rises slowly until around weeks 25–29 when there is a noticeable positive spike in the exit rate. There is a decline after the spike and then another positive spike at weeks 35–39. That these spikes correspond to weeks surrounding the exhaustion of benefits is clear from the very sharp decline in the hazard rate when there is between one and six weeks left until exhaustion.

One question addressed by Meyer is whether the Kaplan–Meier hazard and, in particular the spikes, observed in column 2 are the result of the variation in the length of benefit eligibility in the sample. The idea is to see whether incorporating search model variables, including the level and length of UI benefits, into the baseline hazard shifters, the z's in (23), smooths out the hazard so that there are no longer spikes. It is not necessary to get into details about the exact specification of the exhaustion variable, which is complicated by the fact that for some individuals the eligibility period was extended beyond the original period. Nor are the results of particular concern. Rather, let us turn to more general issues of methodology.

TABLE 2
Unemployement Duration and Time Until Benefits Lapse Hazard Rates[a]

Weeks	Unemployment Duration Hazard	Time Until Benefits Lapse Hazard Rate
1	.082	.165
2	.066	.071
3	.056	.097
4	.061	.070
5	.050	.067
6	.049	.050
7	.042	.052
8	.041	.048
9	.046	.045
10	.037	.056
11	.042	.069
12	.060	.053
13	.061	.059
14	.045	.058
15	.045	.045
16	.041	.035
17	.056	.052
18	.058	.045
19	.047	.050
20	.047	.050
21	.059	.046
22	.058	.058
23	.061	.050
24	.051	.068
25	.079	.071
26	.105	.050
27	.069	.060
28	.095	.050
29	.075	.041
30	.053	.051
31	.040	.053
32	.080	.063
33	.026	.052
34	.045	.061
35	.079	.052
36	.099	.064
37	.057	.065
38	.099	.069

[a] Meyer (1990).

The advantage of this approach over regression is clear. The hazard approach, and in particular this semi-parametric formulation, provides a great deal of detail about the transition process out of unemployment, much more than could be gleaned from looking only at the conditional mean duration function. However, the hazard function is an approximation to (6) in the same way as the duration regression is an approximation to (8) and the same principles should be used in assessing its value.

As in the previous studies already discussed, Meyer includes the pre-unemployment (after-tax) wage to capture differences in the mean of the wage offer distribution. The fact that he adopts a hazard approach does not ameliorate the potential bias in the estimated benefit level effect from the use of this proxy. And the same classificatory principles discussed above apply to the other standard regressors in Meyer's analysis: age, race, schooling, marital status, number of dependents, and the state unemployment rate. It may be less clear that proxy variable bias is a relevant consideration for aggregate level variables such as the state unemployment rate. To see its relevance and because the use of variables reflecting aggregate economic conditions is so prevalent in the unemployment duration literature (as it is in many other literatures), it is useful to develop the point.

As with the pre-unemployment wage, the only rationale for the inclusion of aggregate economic conditions is as a proxy for omitted variables; if c, p, μ, T, and r were perfectly measured the effect of the state unemployment rate on duration (the hazard or mean) would be identically zero. The usual argument is that the state unemployment rate captures demand for labor considerations, corresponding in this case to either p or μ. Consider the regression context. Assuming that duration of individual i in (geographic) state j depends only on the cost of search, c_{ij}, and the mean of the individual's wage offer distribution, μ_{ij}, and letting s_j be the unemployment rate in state j, $\bar{c}_j$ the mean cost of search in state j, and $\bar{\mu}_j$ the mean of the wage offer distribution in state j, the following system of equations describes the relevant relationships necessary to estimate the (linearized) mean duration function:

$$d_{ij} = \pi_1 c_{ij} + \pi_2 \mu_{ij} + \epsilon_{ij},$$
$$s_j = \gamma_1 \bar{c}_j + \gamma_2 \bar{\mu}_j + v_j,$$
$$c_{ij} = \bar{c}_j + \omega_{ij}^c$$
$$\mu_{ij} = \bar{\mu}_j + \omega_{ij}^\mu \qquad\qquad (27)$$

The first equation corresponds to the reduced form duration equation as in (11). The state unemployment rate, somewhat heroically, is aggregated linearly in the second equation as a function of the state's mean cost of search and mean wage. The last two equations merely signify that the mean of any individual's cost of search or wage offer is the state average. It is assumed that all error terms in (27) are independent of each other and are orthogonal to all observables. Further, assume that data is available to correctly measure the cost of search for each individual, but no data is available for mean wage offers, thus giving a rationale for the use of the state unemployment rate as a proxy.[29]

In terms of observable variables, the conditional mean duration function is given by

$$d_{ij} = \left(\pi_1 - \frac{\gamma_1}{\gamma_2} \right) c_{ij} + \frac{\pi_2}{\gamma_2} s_j + \frac{\pi_2}{\gamma_2} \left(v_j - \omega_{ij}^c - \gamma_2 \omega_{ij}^\mu \right). \tag{28}$$

As can be seen from (28), including the state unemployment rate alters the interpretation of the coefficient on the cost of search. Rather than estimating π_1, the effect of search costs on expected duration, (28) estimates $\pi_1 - \frac{\gamma_1}{\gamma_2}$. Moreover, the cost of search is not independent of the regression error in (28), which implies that the estimated parameter is a biased estimator of the search cost parameter in (28). The problem in estimating π_1 from the system given by (27) is that the state unemployment rate is itself determined by the (mean) cost of search, that is, $\gamma_1 \neq 0$, and that the mean cost of search differs across states, that is $\sigma_{\bar{c}_j}^2 \neq 0$. An assumption that $\gamma_1 = 0$ is not plausible because the unemployment rate is the aggregation of individual search decisions. However, while one could argue that search costs do not systematically differ across geographic areas, given the substantial geographic differences in observable mean characteristics such an assumption strikes me as equally implausible.

Even if γ_1 were zero, it is clear from (28) that the effect of the state unemployment rate on unemployment duration would not provide an unbiased estimate of π_2 $\left(\text{or even of its scaled value, } \frac{\pi_2}{\gamma_2} \right)$. To take the extreme case for clarity, suppose that the aggregate variable was the average duration of unemployment in the state rather than the unemployment rate. Then $\gamma_1 = \pi_1$ and $\gamma_2 = \pi_2$. The true coefficient on the average duration variable (s_j) in (28) would be 1, although the estimated value would be less than 1.

In regression models with additive errors the existence of omitted variables that are uncorrelated with included variables has no effect on inference. However, in the hazard approach such omitted variables have inferential consequences. Recalling the discussion of the impact of unobserved heterogeneity on the shape of the population hazard function, because of non-linearities such effects are also transmitted to the included variables even in the proportional hazard model. This fact has led to a large and lively debated literature on alternative methods for incorporating unobserved heterogeneity into hazard models. However, there has been little consideration given to the case where the omitted variables that comprise the unobserved heterogeneity are correlated with the included variables.

In the unemployment duration case, at the very least the pre-unemployment wage will be correlated with individual-specific hetero-geneity. Unless the unobservable is drawn independently in each new unemployment spell, the previous wage, as the outcome of the prior search, will be correlated with it. Individuals with high costs of search will tend to accept low wages in all of their unemployment spells. It is also not very implausible that the unobservable is correlated with many of the pre-determined variables, such as marital status, assets, number of dependents etc. Surely, individuals who draw from wage offer distributions with higher means will make different choices over a whole range of decision variables than will individuals who face lower wage offer means.

2.4.2 Structural Approaches

A major problem with reduced form approaches, as has already been noted, is that the researcher rarely observes the forcing variables faced by individuals, the cost of search, the offer probability, or the wage offer distribution. It is thus not possible to estimate their effects on outcomes of interest unless one is willing to explicitly match them with variables that are observed. The obvious example of such matching is the interpretation of unemployment insurance benefits as a component of the cost of search. However, most other observables have no unambiguous interpretation in terms of the fundamental forcing variables. Yet, the comparative static effects of the forcing variables have clear policy relevance.[30]

One important value of a structural approach is that strict application of economic theory can substitute to some extent for the lack of data. Indeed, the search problem provides one of the nicest examples of the value of economic theory in empirical research. The notion that theory is useful precisely because it places restrictions on what can be observed in the data is well known, if not well enough appreciated. The paper by Lancaster and Chesher (1983) provides one of the clearest presentations of the power of theory.

Lancaster and Chesher exploit answers to the following survey questions asked of a group of unemployed people: (1) How much take home pay would you expect to earn on a new job? (2) Would you tell me the lowest amount you would be prepared to accept? They interpret the answer to the first question as the individual's mean accepted wage, i.e. the expected wage conditional on acceptance as given in (9), and the answer to the second as the reservation wage. They present convincing evidence that these interpretations are plausible. Strictly speaking, they adopt an infinite horizon search model for the analysis.[31]

Table 3 is a slightly modified version of table 1 in Lancaster and Chesher. It expresses comparative static results of changing the level of UI benefits (b) and the offer probability on the reservation wage and on the hazard rate in terms of observables, in this case the mean accepted wage (x), the reservation wage (w^*) and the level of UI benefits. The cost of search is assumed to be negligible relative to the UI benefit level. As Table 3 shows the reservation wage elasticities are independent of the distribution function (F) and of the offered wage, and are bounded between zero and one. The

TABLE 3[a]
Elasticities

Variables	Formula and Bound
$\dfrac{\partial \log w^a}{\partial \log b}$	$0 \leq \dfrac{b}{w^a} \dfrac{x - w^a}{x - b} \leq 1$
$\dfrac{\partial \log w^a}{\partial \log p}$	$0 \leq \dfrac{w^a - b}{w^a} \dfrac{x - w^a}{x - b} \leq 1$
$\dfrac{\partial \log h}{\partial \log b}$	$\dfrac{-f(w^a)b}{1 - F(w^a)} \dfrac{x - w^a}{x - b} \leq 0$
$\dfrac{\partial \log h}{\partial \log p}$	$1 - \dfrac{f(w^a)(w^a - b)}{1 - F(w^a)} \dfrac{x - w^a}{x - b}$

[a] Lancaster and Chesher (1983). Modified Table 1.

hazard rate elasticities depend on the form of the wage offer distribution and only its elasticity with respect to b is constrained (signed).[32]

Thus, although theory alone can provide some policy-relevant estimates, an auxiliary assumption about the form of the wage offer distribution is necessary to provide others. It is remarkable nevertheless how much can be learned by adopting the assumption of optimality. Equally important, the theory can be rejected if the bounds in Table 3 are not satisfied, assuming the subjectively reported reservation wages and mean accepted wages are measured without error. Although Lancaster and Chesher do not report elasticities for each individual, average elasticities always fall within the appropriate bounds within duration groups. The simple search model performs exceedingly well for this particular sample.

The availability of credible subjective data was obviously critical to the Lancaster and Chesher analysis. As already noted, however, such data is not usually available and if one is unwilling to accept the reliability of the data, then the empirical validity of the bounds restrictions can be viewed as a test of the data rather than of the theory. It is therefore useful to consider what can be learned in the more usual case where the available data consist only of observations on unemployment durations and actual accepted wages. Although most data sets also include information on personal characteristics, we will abstract from the use of such data by assuming that the sample is homogeneous in the sense that the individuals face exactly the same values of the (unmeasured) forcing parameters, c, p, F. Now, unlike the case considered by Lancaster and Chesher, the comparative static relationships of interest depend on unmeasured variables. The problem is one of estimation and the primary issue is one of identifiability.

Flinn and Heckman (1982a) provide a rigorous analysis of identification for the infinite horizon search model in which the data consist of duration and accepted wage observations. The arguments, while presented slightly differently, are essentially theirs. It is useful to rewrite the reservation wage equation (5) as

$$w^* = -c + \frac{\beta}{1-\beta} h\left(E\left(w \,\middle|\, w > w^*\right) - w^*\right) \qquad (29)$$

With the available data as described above, the hazard rate and the expected accepted wage can be estimated, the hazard rate from the inverse of mean duration (ignoring the complication of incomplete spells), and the expected accepted wage from the sample mean of accepted wages. Accepted wages are bounded from below by the reservation wage. Thus, as Flinn and Heckman first noted, a consistent estimate of the reservation wage is the lowest observed accepted wage. In addition, if β (the real interest rate) is assumed to be known, then from (29) the cost of search is identified.

This is as far as one can get without making a distributional assumption about F. Even with an estimate of the reservation wage and the hazard rate, p and F are confounded as seen in (6) (ignoring the t subscript). Under some distributional assumptions p and F can be separated. The essential issue is whether the entire wage offer distribution can be recovered from the truncated part of the distribution that is observed. Flinn and Heckman present an example where this recoverability condition is not satisfied, where the distribution is Pareto. Recall that the Pareto distribution is bounded from below by a parameter of the distribution, γ in the prior section. If that parameter is below the reservation wage, then it cannot be recovered from the wage data, although the other Pareto parameter is estimable from the conditional (accepted) wage density.[33] Further, the hazard rate under the Pareto assumption is $\left(\dfrac{p}{\gamma^{\alpha+1}}\right)\left(w^*\right)^{\alpha+1}$, which clearly depends on the unknown Pareto parameter as well as p. The critical assumption, assuming recoverability, is that the reservation wage can be identified from the lowest observed wage. This is a strong assumption given that survey data on wages always appear to contain measurement error. Note, however, that all of the comparative static results shown in Table 3 can be calculated with this data even with the Pareto distribution. As shown in Lancaster and Chesher none of the comparative statics require knowledge of γ. Lancaster and Chesher did not attempt to recover p and F.

The analysis of identification in the finite horizon case is similar. The reservation wage at each duration w_t^* can be estimated consistently from accepted wage data, i.e. as the lowest accepted wage at each duration. Analogous to (29), (4) can be rewritten as

$$w_t^* = -c(1-\beta) + \beta w_{t+1}^* + \beta h_{t+1}\left(E\left(w \mid w > w_{t+1}^*\right) - w_{t+1}^*\right) \qquad (30)$$

Equation (30) must hold exactly. As long as the duration of unemployment exceeds two periods, the finite horizon assumption is sufficient to identify the discount factor, which was not identified in the infinite horizon case, and even without information on T. Moreover, β is overidentified in (30) and the model is, therefore, rejectable. Also, depending on how the terminal condition is modeled, it may be possible to identify all of the parameters, even if the wage distribution is not recoverable. Recall that it was assumed that after the terminal period the reservation wage is zero and any offer would be accepted. Thus, the hazard rate in any period after the terminal period is an estimate of the offer probability. Moreover, in the Pareto case, the lowest observed wage after the terminal period is an estimate of γ.[34]

Engberg (1991) is among the few who has structurally implemented a version of the job search model.[35] Because his goal is the estimation of the effects of unemployment insurance program parameters on unemployment search outcomes, it serves as a useful methodological contrast to the previous papers. Engberg identifies the length of the finite horizon with the length of UI eligibility, which is assumed to be known at the start of the unemployment spell.[36] Until benefits are exhausted the individual solves the finite horizon problem; when benefits are exhausted, the individual solves the infinite horizon problem.

Regardless of the estimation procedure, because all population statistics based on duration and accepted wages depend on reservation wages, as a first step towards estimation it is necessary to solve for the optimal reservation wage path. Given values for c, β, p, and F, the stationary reservation wage after benefit exhaustion can be numerically solved from (5). This stationary reservation wage is the terminal reservation wage, w_T^*, used to solve (4) numerically for $w_{T-1}^* ..., w_1^*$, where $c' = b - c$ replaces c in (4) with b the level of UI benefits.[37]

The usual estimation procedure for structural dynamic discrete choice models has been maximum likelihood.[38] As Flinn and Heckman (1982a) first noted, maximum likelihood in this case is non–standard because the likelihood function must be maximized subject to the inequality constraint that $w_t \geq w_t^*$ (see also Lancaster (1990)). Although such a procedure can be implemented (see Christensen and Kiefer, 1992), the almost certain existence of measurement error in wages makes it unwise to do so. Because the reservation wage is bounded from above by the lowest observed wage, the lowest wage will have an extreme effect on the estimate of the reservation wage. For example, in the Kiefer and Neumann study, the lowest (pre-unemployment) weekly wage was 19 (1967) dollars while in the Meyer study it was 18 (1977) dollars.[39]

Allowing for measurement error in wages, the likelihood function for a sample of I individuals with completed unemployment spell each of length d_i and with observed accepted wage of w_i^0 is

$$\mathscr{L}(\theta) = \prod_{i=1}^{I} \prod_{t=1}^{d_i-1} \left[p_t Pr\left(w_i < w_t^*\right) + \left(1 - p_t\right) \right] p_{d_i} Pr\left(w_i \geq w_{d_i}^*, w_i^o\right), \qquad (31)$$

where the first term in brackets is the probability of remaining unemployed in period t, i.e. of either receiving an unacceptable offer or not receiving an offer, and the second term is the probability of receiving an offer and accepting it and of observing a wage of w^o. The wage offer distribution and the measurement error distribution are both assumed to be log normal. Maximizing the likelihood function with respect to the parameter vector θ, solving for the optimal reservation wage path at each new evaluation, yields consistent and asymptotically normal parameter estimates.

The previous discussion has assumed a homogenous population. Engberg's sample includes individuals of different gender, race, age, education, and family structure. Because of the relatively small sample size, stratification is not feasible. The structural approach requires that one be precise as to where particular observables enter the model. The most general formulation would have the observables shift all of the parameters of the model. Because exclusionary restrictions need not be necessary for identification, it is possible to test where observables should enter.

There is nothing inherent in the structural approach that is informative about appropriate or inappropriate regressors. Engberg allows the pre-unemployment wage to enter the mean of the wage offer distribution (but nowhere else). The strict rationale, however, is not that the pre-unemployment wage is a proxy for the mean, (that is, for omitted skills), but rather that it in fact shifts the mean of the wage offer distribution. As it was previously argued that the pre-unemployment wage would itself be a function of the parameters of the model, having been the outcome of a prior search, assuming no misspecification, a change in the pre-unemployment wage holding those parameters fixed can only be interpreted as a change in the wage offer structure.

If all individuals faced the same benefit exhaustion date, it would be difficult to explain the sharp spikes in the hazard rate at exhaustion dates as observed by Meyer. One could explain such spikes by allowing for the recall of past offers or pre-commitment to begin working after benefits are exhausted, but that would be a different search model. Engberg argues that spikes would arise if there is unobserved heterogeneity. While for any given individual, hazard rates will smoothly increase up to the exhaustion date and thereafter be constant, the existence of unobserved heterogeneity, as previously discussed, will lead to a sample hazard rate that declines after the exhaustion date, thus leading to a spike at the exhaustion date.[40] Engberg allows for unobserved heterogeneity in the mean of the wage offer distribution, in the cost of search, and in the value of leisure. Engberg assumes there to be potentially eight types of individuals in the population and estimates both their separate parameter values and population proportions (see Lancaster and Nickell (1980) and Heckman and Singer (1984)). The likelihood function is a mixture of type-specific likelihood functions of the form given by (31).

While allowing for unobserved heterogeneity may be important in explaining spikes, the assumption that the unobserved heterogeneity distribution is orthogonal to the pre-unemployment wage is not tenable. Individuals with high pre-unemployment wages as an outcome of prior searches are likely to come from the population of individuals with high mean wage offers, low costs of search, and high values of leisure. But, given this correlation, not only does the pre-unemployment wage effect lose its structural interpretation, but so do all of the estimated parameters. If the pre-unemployment wage is believed to shift the current wage offer distribution, then it is necessary to model its determination explicitly. That is, it is necessary to specify in the likelihood function the joint distribution of the pre-unemployment wages and the other unobservables. Such a task would at the very least require information about the number and duration of previous unemployment spells. This is exactly the same problem discussed with Meyer's reduced form; the resolution is also the same. In both cases, the best course, in my view, would be to leave the pre-unemployment wage out of the analysis. The ultimate remedy for omitted variables is to collect better data.

The practical value of the structural approach is that it permits the simulation of policy experiments that are not possible in the reduced form setting. This point is most strikingly illustrated in the context of a homogenous population. Suppose, for example, that all of the individuals in Meyer's sample had faced the same UI program as well as having identical personal characteristics. Meyer's analysis would have consisted then of reporting the baseline hazard. He could not have determined the impact of changes in UI benefits or the benefit horizon on the duration of unemployment distribution. On the other hand, Engberg's analysis would have been essentially unaffected. He could still evaluate the impact on unemployment outcomes of programs to subsidize job search (UI benefit levels and horizons) or of changes in the wage offer distribution (e.g. wage subsidies to unemployed workers). Because the structural approach identifies all of the parameters of the optimization problem, any conceivable policy experiment within the context of the optimization problem can be performed.

But, obviously, Meyer's sample did vary in the UI program parameters they faced. So, if the goal were to evaluate the effect of alternative benefit levels and exhaustion dates on unemployment durations and on accepted wages, which of the two, the reduced form or the structural approach would be preferred? A priori, the answer seems to me unclear if this is the narrow purpose of the analysis.

Without appealing to formal statistical criteria, the answer depends on a subjective judgment as to how well the structural optimization problem fits with one's conception of the actual job search process. It may be that the researcher has misspecified the objective function, some part of the constraint set or the information set. Or, it may be that the optimization problem is correctly specified, but that individuals can only approximate the solution. Or, possibly, individuals approximate the solution to a different optimization problem. The point is that the structural approach may be placing restrictions on behavior that are unwarranted. On the other hand, the reduced form approach, while it may actually correspond to the exact solution of a peculiar optimization problem, is viewed only as an approximation, although supposedly to a wide but unspecified class of models. Given this view of the reduced form, it is unclear how to interpret the estimated effects of the policy variables. Are they to be interpreted as 'average' effects of some kind? Should we use the estimates to extrapolate to policies outside of the observed sample, e.g. discarding UI programs altogether?

We need not rely solely on judgement. One possibility is to compare the performance of alternative models using a goodness-of-fit criterion (see the argument in Heckman and Walker, 1990). In the context of the structural model, comparing predicted vs. actual duration densities is a loose test of the restrictions of the model embedded in the solution for reservation wages (equations (4) and (5)). A more direct method of testing the restrictions of the structural optimization problem, implemented in Wolpin (1987), is to compare the likelihood value for a model in which reservation wages are estimated as separate parameters at each sample duration to the likelihood value of the structural model which restricts the reservation wage path to follow the difference equation (4). The unrestricted or alternative model, however, corresponds to Meyer's estimated non-parametric baseline hazard (not quite exactly because his formulation is in continuous time) in the homogenous population case. By default, Meyer will predict the baseline hazard perfectly while the structural model will not.

Assuming sample variation in UI program parameters, we could compare the fit of Meyer's reduced form under the different unemployment insurance schemes to that of the structural model. But, the semi-parametric form would likely do better given its lack of parsimony. One could, however, again use it as an alternative to the structural null, although it is unclear why a non-parametric alternative stratified by UI parameters wouldn't be preferred.

Possibly a fairer test would be to compare out-of-sample fit where the degrees of freedom issue may be partially ameliorated. Thus, one could estimate the semi-parametric reduced form and the structural model on a sample stratified by UI program parameters, say on the least generous states, and compare their fit to the duration density of the set of more generous states. Unfortunately, such tests have not often appeared in the literature.[41]

A number of the estimated parameters of the search model would seem to have objectively measurable counterparts. Because the parameters are identified using information only on durations and accepted wages, additional data could be used to validate the model. However, there are very few data sets which include information on the receipt of job offers, the wages of rejected offers, or the cost of search. And, there are serious conceptual problems concerning the appropriate measurement of job offers and search costs. To compute an offer probability, is it best to ask a sample of unemployed respondents about all job offers that were received or all offers that could have been received? If, for example, it is observed that individuals mostly accept the first reported offer received, is that simply an outcome of a search process in which formal offers are only solicited if the offer is likely to be accepted, that is, rejections are initiated by the searcher prior to the formal offer? There are no data sets which provide enough detail about the search process to interpret definitively data on rejected job offers. Secondary data, such as that used for most economic analysis, is usually collected without reference to a particular theoretical framework. We, therefore, think very little about the optimal way to connect theory to data.[42]

The general finding of most structural models of job search is that job offer probabilities tend to be low and acceptance rates (reservation wages) high (low). Using different data sets and different formalizations of the job search model, Blau (1991) estimates the offer probability to be about 5 percent per week, Engberg (1991) about 2 percent and Wolpin (1987) about 1 percent per week. Acceptance rates are close to 1 in all of these studies. Thus, independently collected information on the number of rejected offers should show there to be few of them. Using a set of questions about search activities asked in the 1986 and 1987 survey rounds of the NLSY, of the 456 males (age 21–28) who began at least one non-employment spell between the 1985 and 1986 survey rounds, and received at least one offer during the most recent spell, 211 accepted the first offer received. An additional 73 respondents accepted the second offer. Less than 20 percent rejected more than three offers. For the 211 who accepted the first offer, their average duration of unemployment was 3.8 months. In addition, 158 respondents received no offers and had an average (incomplete) spell of 4.7 months (Also see the evidence in Blau and Robbins (1990)).

The reasonably close conformity of the directly measured job offer data with structurally estimated job search parameters does not provide convincing corroborating evidence because of the interpretive difficulties associated with offer data discussed above. This is not to argue that data on offers and, indeed, on the details of the search process, could not be informative. In fact, my view is that only with data of this kind will there be significant further progress in understanding job search behavior.

The job search model clearly is an abstraction in terms of the environment faced by the unemployed searcher. Wages are not the only form of compensation, sometimes offers can be recalled or acceptances delayed, the cost of search depends on the methods of search chosen (e.g. employment agencies, newspapers, friends, etc.), the length of the search horizon may depend on prior savings decisions, etc. Even aside from the 'as if' paradigm, the job search models that have been estimated structurally are surely not accurate representations of behavior in the literal sense. The point of testing the validity of these models is to see to what extent these simplifications matter. Blau (1991), for example, finds that a model in which individuals search jointly over wages and hours, rather than only over wages, fits the data better. There is as yet not enough work, however, to draw strong conclusions about the most promising extensions to pursue, but there are clear directions for further research.

2.4.3 Experimental Approaches

Given the limitations of both the reduced form and structural approaches, a complementary approach is to replicate experimentally the environment of the job search model and determine whether individuals behave in the way predicted by the job search model. A number of experimental studies have been conducted with this goal. The fundamental assumption of this approach is that individuals behave in the artificial environment exactly as they would in the real world if the real world matched the artificial one. Schotter and Braunstein (1981) provide an excellent illustration of the experimental method.

Schotter and Braunstein conduct an experiment which corresponds to the search model with a unitary offer probability. Individuals (56 NYU undergraduates) draw repeatedly from a known (to them, as well as to the researcher) wage offer distribution at a fixed cost per draw and can stop drawing at any time. They are paid the wage they accept minus total search costs. The 'infinite' horizon experiment allows them to draw indefinitely while the finite horizon experiment fixes the number of allowable draws at the start. They test a number of job search predictions and generally find them in agreement with the observed behavior. It is of interest to consider a few of these tests.

One hypothesis they test is that individuals actually behave according to a reservation wage rule and that, if they do, they use the correct reservation wage. To test this hypothesis, Schotter and Braunstein first asked each player what wage they would accept not to play the game. In the infinite horizon case, this should correspond to the reservation wage. They find that the average reported reservation wage is very close to the theoretically correct reservation wage that is obtained as the solution to equation (5) given the known parameters.[43] In further support of the hypothesis it was found that the average highest rejected wage offer was below the optimal reservation wage and the average actual accepted wage offer was below the optimal reservation wage and the average actual accepted wage was not very different from the expected accepted wage conditional on the reported reservation wage. A second hypothesis concerns the behavioral reaction to changes in the cost of search. As predicted by the job search model, a rise in the cost of search reduced (significantly, in a statistical sense) the reservation wage. However, the average accepted wage rose although the increase was not statistically significant.

The Schotter–Braunstein study tends to support the view that in a laboratory setting individuals do follow the optimal stopping rule. This is generally the finding of the handful of other experimental studies of job search behavior.[44] If it is assumed that individuals play the game seriously, then rejection of the job search model in the artificial environment would seem to imply that structural estimation of the job search model would be only of methodological interest. Indeed, a true believer in the experimental approach might take non-rejection as a necessary condition for non-experimental empirical work that is founded on the optimal stopping paradigm. Such an argument is incomplete, however, without having an explicit loss function to assess the damage from using a misspecified model.

Experimental work cannot be used for policy analysis because the parameters faced by individuals in the real market are unknown; thus, the critical role for estimation using market generated data. However, the experimental approach and estimation are not as disconnected as this argument makes it appear. Once it is recognized that the data generated by experiments are nonetheless data, the experimental approach can be exploited to improve the estimation outcome. Just as with the non-experimental job search data used in estimation, experimental studies such as Schotter and Braunstein's also generate information on completed durations of unemployment and on accepted wages. That data can be used to estimate reduced form and structural models. The opportunities are numerous. Among the most salient questions that could be addressed are: (1) How closely do reduced form parameters correspond to average population effects? (2) How much do parameter estimates obtained from the structural model differ from the true parameters? How much does using additional information such as rejected offers improve the estimates? (3) Do reduced form or structural approaches provide better estimates of policy effects? (4) What effect does using an incorrect distributional assumption for wage offers have on the structural estimates? Notice that the reduced form may outperform the structural model because the structural model is not literally true.[45] In the Schotter and Braunstein study, reservation wages are not chosen optimally except on average. Further, the structural model can be estimated with only the partial information that is usually available, for example, using accepted but not rejected wage offers. This synergy between 'experimentalists' and 'estimators' has yet to be exploited.

2.5 An Equilibrium Two-State Search Model

The partial equilibrium job search model can be used to determine the impact of alternative government interventions on search outcomes only if the effect of the policies on market determined parameters are known. The analysis of policy effects, such as changes in UI parameters, thus requires an equilibrium framework. Changes in IU benefits, for example, likely will alter the distribution of wage offers and the probability of receiving offers. There has been very little work on the estimation of equilibrium search models which have as the worker's optimization problem, the standard job search model, even though the theoretical literature is fairly large.[46] An exception is the paper by Eckstein and Wolpin (1990).

The paper by Eckstein and Wolpin has two purposes: (1) to explore the feasibility of estimating a search equilibrium model using information only on workers and not firms; and (2) to see to what extent the equilibrium model can account for the dispersion of observed wages. The relevance of this latter goal is that an important motivation for the development of equilibrium search models was to demonstrate the theoretical possibility of generating equilibrium wage dispersion when, as assumed in the standard job search model, workers are homogenous in terms of productivity.

The basis for the Eckstein and Wolpin paper is the model by Albrecht and Axell (1984). In that model individuals work in a market where firms differ in their productivity, although all workers would have the same productivity at the same firm that is, workers are homogenous with respect to their market skills. Workers are, however, heterogenous with respect to their non-market productivity (or preferences for leisure). Individual preferences and firm productivities are private information, but the distributions of preferences and productivities over individuals and firms, respectively, are known to all agents. A Nash equilibrium wage offer distribution exists that corresponds to the reservation wages of workers with the appropriately solved wage offer probability distribution. The wage offer distribution is a function of both the worker preference distribution for leisure and the firm productivity distribution.

It is useful in developing the estimation method to outline the structure of the model. In each period new individuals, who live forever, enter and exit the labor market. The constant exit rate is τ; the entry rate will be given below. Each individual of a particular entry cohort solves a standard infinite horizon search model modified by the existence of the exogenous exit rate and by a lump sum dividend that is invariant to employment status. There are $n+1$ types of individuals who differ according to their per-period non-market value of time, z_j, $j = 0, ..., n$; $z_{j+1} > z_j$. The solution to each of the worker type's optimization problem is characterized by a reservation wage, w_j^*.

Now, the Nash equilibrium solution turns out to be a wage offer distribution that is discrete such that $w_{i-1} < w_i < w_{i+1}$ with probabilities γ_i, $i = 0, ..., n$. Moreover, the equilibrium set of wage offers is equal to the set of reservation wages, that is, $w_j^* = w_j$ for all j. There are, thus, as many wages as there are reservation wages. Letting $\gamma^j = \sum_{i=0}^{j-1} \gamma_i$ be the probability of receiving an offer of $w < w_j$, given that an offer is received, the solution to the set of reservation wages is

$$w_j = \omega_1 z_j + \omega_2 \sum_{i=j+1}^{n} \gamma_i w_i,$$

$$w_n = z_n, \tag{32}$$

where $\omega_1 + \omega_2 = 1$ are weights that depend on the discount factor (β), the offer probability (p), τ and γ^{j+1}.[47] Thus, the reservation wage of type j is a weighted average of type j's value of leisure and the mean (reservation) wage over the types with higher values of leisure than j. Clearly, $w_{j+1} > w_j$ for all j.

Each of the F potential firms (F large) faces a linear production technology.

$$y = \lambda \ell, \tag{33}$$

where y is output, ℓ is the number of workers, and $\lambda \geq 0$ is a firm-specific productivity (managerial capability) index that comes from a continuous distribution function $A(\lambda)$ with $A(0) = 0$. The firm maximizes period-specific profits

$$\pi(w, \lambda) = (\lambda - w)\ell(w), \tag{34}$$

where $\ell(w)$ is the supply of workers to the firm when wage w is offered. Firms take the $\ell(w)$ function as given and offer a wage from among the equilibrium set, $w_0, w_1, ..., w_n$, that maximizes profits. Then,

$$\lambda_j = \frac{w_j \ell(w_j) - w_{j-1} \ell(w_{j-1})}{\ell(w_j) - \ell(w_{j-1})} \tag{35}$$

is a critical value of λ which makes a firm indifferent between offering w_j or w_{j-1}. A firm with a value of λ between λ_j and λ_{j+1} will offer a wage w_j and, because w_0 is the lowest wage, $\lambda_0 = w_0$ is the lowest productivity associated with an active firm, that is, a firm capable of earning positive profits. $A(w_0)$ is the proportion of potential firms that are inactive.

To solve for the equilibrium requires that $\ell(w_j)$ be determined. Letting β_j be the proportion of workers of type j and k the total number of workers in the market, assume that $\tau k \beta_j$ new workers enter the market each period. Then the proportion of total workers per firm offering w_j is

$$\ell(w_j) = \sum_{r=0}^{j} \frac{\mu \beta_r p}{\left(1 - (1-p) + p\gamma^r\right)(1-\tau)}, \tag{36}$$

where $\mu = \dfrac{k}{F(1 - A(\lambda_0))}$ is the number of workers per active firm. The labor supply calculation is made at the steady state of the economy where there are infinitely many past cohorts of new entrants to the market. Finally, the probability of receiving an offer p is assumed to be an increasing function of the number of active firms per worker, i.e.,

$$p = G\left(\frac{1}{\mu(\lambda_0)}\right), G' > 0, \tag{37}$$

where G is a technological function capturing the notion that workers sample from the distribution of potential forms but only obtain an offer when they meet an active firm.[48]

The Nash equilibrium is the probability density function

$$\gamma_j = \frac{A(\lambda_{j+1}) - A(\lambda_j)}{1 - A(\lambda_0)}, \qquad j = 0, 1, \ldots, n-1, \tag{38}$$

where the γ_j's are the proportions of active firms offering wage w_j, $\sum_{j=0}^{n} \gamma_j = 1$, and where the reservation wages, the λ_j's and the labor supplies are determined by the above equations.[49] Upon substituting (32) and (36) into (35), and the resulting expression for the λ_j's and $\lambda_0 = w_0$ from (32) into (37) and (38), yields a system of equations of the form

$$\gamma_0 = \gamma_0\left(\gamma_0, \gamma_1, \ldots, \gamma_n, p\right)$$

$$\gamma_1 = \gamma_1\left(\gamma_0, \gamma_1, \ldots, \gamma_n, p\right)$$

$$\vdots \qquad \vdots$$

$$\gamma_{n-1} = \gamma_{n-1}\left(\gamma_0, \gamma_1, \ldots, \gamma_n, p\right)$$

$$\gamma_n = \gamma_n\left(\gamma_0, \gamma_1, \ldots, \gamma_n, p\right)$$

$$p = p\left(\gamma_0, \gamma_1, \ldots, \gamma_n, p\right) \tag{39}$$

with $\sum_{j=0}^{n} \gamma_j = 1, 0 \leq \gamma_j, p \leq 1$. Given values for the fundamental parameters of the model, namely, the β_j's, the z_j's, $A(\lambda)$, $G(\cdot)$, τ, and β, equation (39) can be numerically solved for the γ_j's and for p.[50]

The model generates an equilibrium distribution of unemployment duration for any new cohort of labor market entrants. Allowing d to be the duration of unemployment (search), then the probability that a randomly selected individual will begin employment in period $d + 1$ (at $t = d$) is

$$f_d = \sum_{j=0}^{n} (1 - \tau)^d \left[p\gamma^j + (1 - p) \right]^d p\left(1 - \gamma^j\right)\beta_j. \tag{40}$$

Equation (40) is the probability that an individual survives d periods, either does not receive an offer or rejects an offer for d periods, and receives and accepts an offer at $t = d$, averaged over the $n + 1$ types in the population. It is a mixture (over types) of $n + 1$ negative binomial distributions. The hazard rate at $t = d$, the conditional probability of leaving unemployment after d periods, is by definition

$$h_d = \frac{f_d}{(1 - \tau)^d \prod_{k=1}^{d-1} \left(1 - h_k\right)}. \tag{41}$$

As previously noted, it is a well-known result that the population hazard rate is decreasing in duration due to heterogeneity, exhibiting negative duration dependence even though each type has a constant hazard rate $p\,(1 - \gamma^j)$. Both

(40) and (41) depend on the fundamental parameters of the model through the equilibrium determination of the γ_j's and p.[51]

Suppose we have a sample of I individuals who enter the market at a point in time and are followed until a job offer is received and accepted. Then the likelihood function is

$$L = \prod_{i=1}^{I} f_{d_i} \tag{42}$$

where f_{d_i} is given by (40). Now (42) can serve as the basis for estimation of either an unrestricted version of the equilibrium model (with $\tau = 0$), that is, with parameters p, and the γ_j's and the β_j's, or of the (restricted) equilibrium model which imposes restrictions across the γ_j's and p according to (39) based on the fundamental parameters.

The unrestricted model contains $2n + 1$ parameters (n free γ's, n free β's, and p). Identification of the mixture model has been established. Note that unlike the standard search model in which p is not identified from duration data alone, because $\gamma^0 = 0$, that is, the lowest z-type always accepts an offer when received, p is identified.[52]

Given that the γ_j's and p are identified in the unrestricted model, the question is whether the 'structural' parameters can be identified from them. Because of the non-linear nature of (39), this is a difficult question to answer. Eckstein and Wolpin simply impose sufficient restrictions so that there are as many parameters as equations.[53] The counting requirement is that $n \geq r + q + 2$ where n is the number of types less one, q is the number of parameters in Λ (λ), and r is the order of the polynomial

$$z_j - z_{j-1} = \left| \alpha_0 + \alpha_1 j + \alpha_2 j^2 + \dots, + \alpha_r j^r \right| \tag{43}$$

where z_0 is normalized and δ is fixed. With $q = 2$ and $r = 2$, there must be 7 types of individuals in order to satisfy the inequality restriction. The more types of individuals there actually are in the population, the more likely are necessary and sufficient conditions to be satisfied with a given parameterization, that is, a given q and r.[54]

The point is that it is feasible to estimate the parameters of an equilibrium model including those of firms using data only on a single cohort of new worker entrants. Whether such a strategy is useful for policy depends in part on the empirical performance of the model. The conclusion from this one study is that it is not. Neither the unrestricted nor the equilibrium model fits the duration data well and the equilibrium model's fit is particularly poor. Of more significance is that the equilibrium model cannot generate even a small proportion of the observed wage variance in the data, which was one of the original goals of equilibrium search models.

The Albrecht and Axell model is not the only framework that can generate equilibrium wage dispersion, but that is not the issue in my view. The endemic problem in estimating such models is the extreme paucity of data. The Eckstein and Wolpin effort is a demonstration of structure substituting for data in an extreme form. It will be impossible to compare alternative equilibrium formulations with any statistical power if the only data that is available is that on workers. As with the partial equilibrium search model, a much more intensive data collection effort is required.[55]

3. THE THREE-STATE JOB SEARCH MODEL

The two-state search model assumes there to be a distinct unemployment state in which individuals expend resources on identifying job vacancies and receive offers when successful. Extended versions of the standard model allow individuals to choose the intensity of search. If, in addition, non-market time has value, it is possible that an individual will choose to expend no resources on search activities (Burdett and Mortensen, 1978). This framework is a natural conceptual underpinning for the labor force participation dichotomy. Individuals who spend no resources on job search while not employed are out-of-the labor force.

The Current Population Survey distinguishes between out-of-the labor force and unemployed respondents by asking respondents who were not working during the survey week whether they 'engaged in any specific job seeking activity within the past four weeks.' Because what constitutes a 'job search activity' is not precisely defined, there is some doubt about whether this question identifies a real behavioral distinction between the two non-employment states (Clark and Summers (1982), Ellwood (1982)).

There is evidence in the job search data of the NLSY's 1986 and 1987 interviews previously described that the CPS-style question may lead to misclassification. At the time of the 1986 survey all male respondents who had experienced at least one non-employment spell since the 1985 survey were asked whether or not they were looking for work during none, some, or all of the weeks of their most recent non-employment spell. Respondents who stated that they had looked for work during some or all of the period were then asked a battery of questions about their specific search activities. The 1987 survey round continued this battery for those respondents who had not completed their spell by the 1986 survey. The battery of questions included a list of ten specific search activities (and an 'other' category) from which a respondent could choose as describing their search behavior in each separate month of non-employment. The last option on the list was no method used or not looking for work in that month.

The data reveal that of 1032 high school graduates who had a non-employment spell and who had stated that they had looked for work during some or all of the weeks of the spell, 334 listed 'no method' as descriptive of their search activity in each month of the spell. Thus 32 percent of the respondents who would have been classified as unemployed according to the looking-for-work criterion would more correctly be classified as out-of-the labor force if based on their specific search activities. Moreover, this figure probably underestimates the extent of misclassification because some individuals who had reported not having looked for work, when prompted with a list of specific search methods might have reported some search behavior. The CPS question may be somewhat better at classification than the NLSY question given its mention of 'specific job seeking activity' as opposed to the NLSY's 'looking for work', but the NLSY evidence seems to make an *a priori* case for studying the issue.

It is useful in developing ways to test for the existence of separate non-employment states to write down a formal three-state behavioral model. Letting V^e, V^u, and V^o be the value functions associated with the employment, unemployment and out-of-the labor force states, and allowing for a monetary value of non-market time in the two non-employment states, b^u and b^o, a straightforward extension of the infinite horizon two-state model is to write the value function as

$$V^e(w) = w + \beta V^e(w),$$

$$V^u = b^u - c + \beta\left[p^u E \max\left(V^e, V^u, V^o\right) + \left(1 - p^u\right) E \max\left(V^u, V^o\right)\right],$$

$$V^o = b^o + \beta\left[p^o E \max\left(V^e, V^u, V^o\right) + \left(1 - p^o\right) E \max\left(V^u, V^o\right)\right], \qquad (44)$$

where it is assumed that there may be a positive probability of receiving an offer p^o even when not spending resources on search. In the three-state model, it is assumed that the wage distribution is state-dependent, that is wage offers depend on which of the two non-employment states the individual occupied in the previous period. The distribution functions are denoted by F^u and F^o. In addition, it is assumed that b^u and b^o are random, thus allowing for probabilistic transitions between the non-employment states.

This model assumes that there are distinct non-employment states recognized by individuals. So, while the model may capture the behavioral decision process, it does not encompass the notion of reporting ambiguity that led researchers to question the operational distinction. To capture the potential ambiguity of CPS-type self-reported non-employment states, define the value of reporting being unemployed as $\tilde{V}^u = V^u + v^u$ and that of being out-of-the labor force $\tilde{V}^o = V^o + v^o$, where V^o and V^u are (possibly time-varying) non-zero bias terms induced by the ambiguity of the survey question. The idea is that individuals may attach a higher or lower value to reporting particular non-employment states. But, it should be recognized that the individual maximizes wealth by solving (44) for the stationary value functions, V^o, V^u, and V^e and choosing the state according to which is the highest. The individual only reports their decision based on $\tilde{V}^o$ and $\tilde{V}^e$.

Now, it is reasonable to adopt the definition that the two non-employment states would be equivalent if the value functions were identical. A sufficient condition for $V^u = V^o$ is that $p^u = p^o$, $F^u = F^o$, and $b^u - c = b^o$. To see the data implications of equivalence, consider first the transition probabilities from unemployment to employment (P_{ue}) and from out-of-the labor force to employment (P_{oe}). Letting $P_e(j) = Pr\left(V^e > V^u, V^e > V^o \mid j\right)$, $j = u, o$, be the probability of choosing employment conditional on having been in state j the previous period and conditional on having received an offer, these transition probabilities can be written as:

$$P_{ue} = \frac{\pi^u P_e(u) p^u \left[Pr\left(\tilde{V}^u > \tilde{V}^o \mid V^u > V^o\right)\right] + \pi^o P_e(o) p^o \left[Pr\left(\tilde{V}^u > \tilde{V}^o \mid V^o > V^u\right)\right]}{Pr\left(\tilde{V}^u > \tilde{V}^o\right)};$$

$$P_{oe} = \frac{\pi^u P_e(u) p^u \left[Pr\left(\tilde{V}^o > \tilde{V}^u \mid V^u > V^o\right)\right] + \pi^o P_e(o) p^o \left[Pr\left(\tilde{V}^o > \tilde{V}^u \mid V^o > V^u\right)\right]}{Pr\left(\tilde{V}^o > \tilde{V}^u\right)}.$$

(45)

P_{ue} is the probability that an individual is actually in u (π^u), receives and accepts an offer ($P_e(u)p^u$), and reports being in u, plus the probability that an individual is actually in o (π^o), receives and accepts an offer ($P_e(o)p^o$), and reports being in u, divided by the probability the individual reports being in u. P_{oe} is similarly obtained. As (45) shows, the two will generally not be the same.

When the two non-employment states are equivalent, $P_e(u) = P_e(o) = P_e$ and $p^u = p_o = p$. In this case, (45) reduces to

$$P_{ue} = pP_e,$$
$$P_{oe} = pP_e. \tag{46}$$

Thus, with equivalence, the transition to employment is the same regardless of the origin of the non-employment state.

Transitions between non-employment states are significantly more complicated than those to employment shown in (45) in the general case of non-equivalence. However, equivalence is not sufficient for transitions between all non-employment states to be equal. In particular,

$$P_{uo} = \frac{\left[p(1-P_e)+(1-p)\right]\left[\pi^u Pr\left(\tilde{V}^o > \tilde{V}^u, > \tilde{V}^u > V^o \middle| V^u > V^o\right) + \pi^o Pr\left(\tilde{V}^o > \tilde{V}^u, > \tilde{V}^u > \tilde{V}^o \middle| V^o > V^u\right)\right]}{Pr\left(\tilde{V}^o > \tilde{V}^u\right)},$$

$$P_{uu} = \frac{\left[p(1-P_e)+(1-p)\right]\left[\pi^u Pr\left(\tilde{V}^u > \tilde{V}^o, > \tilde{V}^u > \tilde{V}^o \middle| V^u > V^o\right) + \pi^o Pr\left(\tilde{V}^u > \tilde{V}^o, > \tilde{V}^u > \tilde{V}^o \middle| V^o > V^u\right)\right]}{Pr\left(\tilde{V}^u > \tilde{V}^o\right)},$$

$$P_{uo} = \frac{\left[p(1-P_e)+(1-p)\right]\left[\pi^u Pr\left(\tilde{V}^u > \tilde{V}^o, > \tilde{V}^o > \tilde{V}^u \middle| V^u > V^o\right) + \pi^o Pr\left(\tilde{V}^u > \tilde{V}^o, > \tilde{V}^o > \tilde{V}^u \middle| V^o > V^u\right)\right]}{Pr\left(\tilde{V}^o > \tilde{V}^u\right)},$$

$$P_{uo} = \frac{\left[p(1-P_e)+(1-p)\right]\left[\pi^u Pr\left(\tilde{V}^o > \tilde{V}^u, > \tilde{V}^o > \tilde{V}^u \middle| V^o > V^o\right) + \pi^o Pr\left(\tilde{V}^o > \tilde{V}^u, > \tilde{V}^o > \tilde{V}^u \middle| V^o > V^u\right)\right]}{Pr\left(\tilde{V}^o > \tilde{V}^u\right)}. \tag{47}$$

In general, all of these transition probabilities will differ. In the special case where reporting bias is independent over periods, i.e. there are no permanent individual effects, transition probabilities are independent of the origin state, $P_{uo} = P_{oo}$ and $P_{ou} = P_{uu}$. However, even in this case, transition probabilities need not be symmetric, that is, P_{uo} need not equal P_{ou}.

One method of testing the distinctness hypothesis would be to estimate the structural three-state model and test the parameter restrictions that would ensure that $V^o = V^u$. However, data on only accepted wages and on the sequence of non-employment states would not be sufficient to identify the parameters of the structural model. The insight of Flinn and Heckman to use the lowest accepted wage as an estimate of the reservation wage doesn't carry over to the three-state model where there are multiple reservation wages. The direct measurement of offer probabilities would seem to be required at the least, but distinguishing between the values of non-market time and systematic reporting bias would seem impossible without detailed data on actual search activities.

As first noted by Flinn and Heckman (1983) the implications of equivalence, shown in (46), can be tested. For a homogenous population, equivalence implies that the transition to employment will be independent of the origin state. As they note, however, the test does not distinguish between alternative sources of non-equivalence. Distinctness can arise because any of the equivalence restrictions are violated. It is also true that one may fail to reject equivalence when it is in fact false. Offer probabilities, wage offer distributions, and values of non-market time may be different in such a way that P_{ue} and P_{oe} are statistically indistinguishable.

The 1986 and 1987 NLSY survey rounds may be the only large scale data that distinguishes unemployment and out-of-the labor force states during a non-employment spell. Pooling all periods, for white (male) high school graduates the proportion of out-of-the labor force periods (months) followed directly by employment is .14 while the proportion of unemployed spells followed by employment is .21. Similarly, for blacks, the respective figures are .07 and .18. This evidence, that unemployment more often precedes employment than does out-of-the labor force, is also found when the empirical hazard functions are compared for those who searched each period of their non-employment spell vs. those who were out-of-the labour force in every period. As Table 4 shows, except for the first period, the hazard rate for the unemployed group exceeds that for the out-of-the labor force group.

This analysis is obviously only suggestive and the data awaits a full exploration. Flinn and Heckman (1983) estimated a reduced form hazard, allowing for a time-varying covariate (marital status) and for unobserved heterogeneity using an earlier data source (the young men's cohort of the NLS). Gonul (1992) extended their analysis using earlier rounds of the NLSY. Flinn and Heckman found that unemployment and out-of-the labor force were distinct states, while Gonul found them to be distinct for females but not for males.[56] The issue remains open.

TABLE 4

Kaplan–Meier Non-Employment Hazard Rates

By Non-Employment State and by Race[a]

DURATION (months)	WHITE		BLACK	
	Unemployed [b]	Out-of-the Labor Force [c]	Unemployed [b]	Out-of-the Labor Force [c]
1	0.128	0.132	0.053	0.083
2	0.312	0.264	0.228	0.186
3	0.205	0.163	0.196	0.093
4	0.204	0.149	0.184	0.068
5	0.243	0.117	0.114	0.054
6	0.231	0.161	0.146	0.049
7	0.085	0.111	0.122	0.050
8	0.177	0.075	0.129	0.046
9	0.167	0.108	0.157	0.055
10	0.194	0.048	0.119	0.067
11	0.115	0.052	0.133	0.063
12	0.333	0.143	0.348	0.038
13	0.091	0.082	0.125	0.039
14	0.111	0.136	0.143	0.01
15	0.0	0.079	0.0	0.045
16	0.25	0.0	0.167	0.036

[a] Source: Kum (1992).

[b] Searched in each month of the non-employment spell.

[c] Did not search in any month of the non-employment spell.

4. JOB TURNOVER AND THE WAGE-TENURE RELATIONSHIP

People do change employers, so a natural extension of the job search model is to drop the assumption that jobs last forever. There are, however, a number of plausible reasons why individuals change jobs. They may receive a better wage offer, their current wage may fall (relative, say, to the value they attach to leisure), they may acquire information which leads them to reassess (downward) their productivity with the firm, or they may be permanently laid off. There is an extensive theoretical literature which builds many of these features, generally singly, into the job search framework. All of these models have essentially the same qualitative predictions. This common feature of their comparative statics (dynamics) does not imply, however, that they are observationally equivalent, i.e. that the data that would reject any one of them would reject all of them. However, it does imply that distinguishing between the models might not be easy.

4.1 A Simple Model of Job Turnover

Job turnover models not only have predictions about the determinants of the rate of job leaving, but also about the relationship between wages and job tenure (duration). To see that, consider the simplest job turnover model, one in which new job offers are received while employed with probability p per period.[57] Letting $V(w)$ be the value of a job with wage w, it can be written as

$$V(w) = w + \beta \left[pE \max \left(V(x), V(w) \right) + (1 - p)V(w) \right] \qquad (48)$$

If an offer is received an individual chooses between the current wage and the new wage offer (x), while if no offer is received the individual continues to work at the current wage. The obvious implication of this model is that only new wage offers that exceed the current wage will be accepted, that is, the reservation wage is equal to the current wage.

Now, suppose one has data on the completed tenure of the first job, on the wage of that job in the last employment period, and on the wage of the new job for a homogenous population, that is, for a population with the same initial job reservation wage. Although this particular configuration of data is somewhat contrived, it enables one to abstract from the distinction between total work experience and tenure on a particular job and facilitates the general point. Given that individuals exit from their first job based on whether a new job offer exceeds their current wage, those who exit earlier will on average have had lower initial wage draws. Thus there will be a positive correlation in the data between tenure and the terminal wage. The hazard (exit) rate is in fact $h = p(1-F(w))$ where F is the wage offer distribution function and w is the current wage. Expected duration is h^{-1} and so completed tenure for individual i is

$$T_i = g(w,p) + u_i, \qquad (49)$$

where $\dfrac{\partial T_i}{\partial w} > 0$. An alternative explanation for the observed positive wage-tenure relationship is that workers accumulate human capital on-the-job, that is,

$$w_i = \overline{w}\left(T_i\right) + \epsilon_i. \tag{50}$$

Assuming that $\overline{w}(0) \neq 0, \epsilon_i$ can be assumed to have zero mean with variance equal to the variance of F. Clearly, any attempt to estimate $\overline{w}(T_i)$ from (5) using the available data will overstate the effect of tenure on wages.

Given the strong prediction of the job turnover model that any acceptable wage at a new employer must exceed the current wage, the job turnover model would be rejected if that restriction were violated for any observation. Suppose that wages were perfectly measured and that the restriction was in fact not universally valid. Clearly, we should reject the job turnover model as stated. Of course, it would not be appropriate, therefore, to regard (50) as the true model of the wage-tenure relationship because the test of the job turnover model did not take that as the specific alternative.

However, one can test the specific alternative that $w(T)$ exists by nesting the two models in the more general combined model, namely one which individuals continue to receive offers while employed and wages rise with job tenure. In this model, the value of being employed with initial wage draw ϵ given tenure T is

$$V(\epsilon, T) = \overline{w}(T) + \epsilon + \beta\Big[pE\max\big(V(\epsilon, T+1), V(\epsilon', 0)\big) + (1-p)V(\epsilon, T+1)\Big] \tag{51}$$

where ϵ' is the alternative random wage draw over which the expectation is taken. Clearly, the value of employment at a firm increases with T (a firm is defined by its ϵ draw) as long as $\overline{w}(T)$ is increasing in T. Thus, the reservation wage draw, that is, the ϵ, necessary to induce a job match increases with tenure; the hazard rate is decreasing in T. But, as in the original job turnover model without true wage growth, the reservation wage draw also increases with the current wage, ϵ, thus imparting a behaviorally induced positive correlation between tenure and wages.

Recall that the model without wage growth had the implication that a new wage offer would be acceptable only if it exceeded the old wage. With wage growth, this may no longer be the case and depends on the shape of the wage-tenure relationship. The same result would occur only if the wage-tenure relationship were linear or convex, while accepted wages could be below the old wage if the $w(T)$ function were concave.

Although actually solving the individual's optimization problem is somewhat complicated by the fact that ϵ is a component of the state space and is a continuous variable, the solution, for given parameter values p, β, F, and those of the $\overline{w}(T)$ function, consists of a sequence of reservation draws, $\epsilon^*(1,\epsilon)$, ..., $\epsilon^*(T,\epsilon)$, ..., which equate the stationary value functions $V(\epsilon, T)$ to $V(\epsilon^*(T, \epsilon), 0)$. Those reservation draws are the levels of ϵ that make the individual indifferent between remaining at the same employer or accepting a new offer. As already noted, if the wage function is globally concave, accepted wages may be below current wages. In fact, using previous arguments, the lowest accepted wage at each completed tenure is a consistent estimate of the reservation wage $\left(\overline{w}(0) + \epsilon^*(T, \epsilon)\right)$. If the distribution function F is recoverable, then both its parameters and the offer probability p is identified. Fixing β (whether it is identified is unclear), then the set of $\epsilon^*(T, \epsilon)$'s and the data on current wages and completed tenure can be used to estimate the parameters of $w(T)$. Given the parameters, one can determine the extent to which the positive wage-tenure correlation is due to optimal job turnover and the extent to which it is due to skill acquisition.

The literature on estimating wage-tenure functions has been concerned with alternative explanations for the relationship that go beyond the simple turnover model presented above. Quite clever methods have been posited for eliminating the bias in that relationship induced by behavior (see, for example, Altonji and Shakotko (1987), Abraham and Farber (1987), or Topel (1991)). However, none of these methods accounts for all of the confounding behaviors that are plausible. A promising approach, in my view, would be, as in the previous illustration, to embed the human capital wage function in a comprehensive behavioral model and to estimate the structure jointly. A useful comparison can be made between the two approaches.

4.2. Approaches to Estimating The Wage-Tenure Relationship

4.2.1 Topel's Two-Step Procedure

Topel (1991) exemplifies a non-structural approach broadly consistent with theory and designed to address the single question of whether there is an economic return to job tenure. Topel considers the prototypical model of wage determination

$$\ln w_{ijt} = X_{ijt}\beta_1 + T_{ijt}\beta_2 + \epsilon_{ijt}, \tag{52}$$

where w_{ijt} is the wage that individual i receives on job j at time t, X_{ijt} is total labor market experience, and T_{ijt} is job tenure or seniority. The point of the paper is to estimate the parameters of (52). The estimation problem concerns the fact that the unobservable in (52) may be correlated with work experience and with tenure due to optimizing behavior on the part of workers (as for example described above). Topel decomposes the wage error into three mutually orthogonal parts, one that is specific to a worker-firm match (ϕ_{ijt}), one that is specific only to the worker (μ_i), and one that is related to random shocks in the market and/or measurement error (v_{ijt}). Concentrating on the correlation between the match-specific component and the experience regressors in (52), Topel shows that under the simple selection rule of choosing the job with the highest wage (1) the bias in the effect of total work experience on wages is positive, but (2) the bias in the tenure effect is negative if there is in fact a true (positive) tenure effect on wages. The reason for the latter result is that the stayers, those with longer tenure, need not have as good matches when there is positive wage growth with tenure, while the movers need to have even better matches to compensate for the loss in tenure. It is a corollary that the sum of the two effects is biased upwards. While the negative bias in the tenure effect does not necessarily survive with embellishments to the underlying turnover model, the point is that one cannot say *a priori* that cross-sectional regression estimates that fail to take into account selective turnover necessarily overstate the return to job tenure.

Topel suggests a two-step estimator. Differencing (52) at two points in time for persons who do not change jobs yields

$$\ln w_{ijt} - \ln w_{ijt'} = (\beta_1 + \beta_2)(t - t') + \epsilon_{ijt} - \epsilon_{ijt'}. \tag{53}$$

If aside from fixed job- and individual-specific characteristics, job changing is random, i.e. if the difference in the random wage draws have zero mean conditional on choosing to be in the same job at the two points in time, then estimation of (53) by ordinary least squares will provide a consistent estimate of the sum of the total experience and tenure effects. To separately estimate the two effects, a second regression is estimated that is derived from the fact that total experience on any job is the sum of the initial experience upon starting the job and tenure on that job. Substituting that identity into (52) gives

$$\ln w - (\beta_1 + \beta_2) T = X_0 \beta_1 + \epsilon. \tag{54}$$

The regression is estimated using the first stage consistent estimate of $\beta_1 + \beta_2$. However, as Topel notes, new jobs are not randomly selected so that initial experience (X_0) is likely to be correlated with the error in (54), that is, the wage at which one is willing to switch to a new job will depend on the amount of total work experience the individual has at that time. Thus, β_1 cannot be consistently estimated from (54). The expected value of the two step estimator of each parameter is

$$E\beta_1 = \beta_1 + b_1 + \gamma_{X_0 T} (b_1 + b_2)$$
$$E\beta_2 = \beta_2 + b_1 + \gamma_{X_0 T} (b_1 + b_2), \tag{55}$$

where b_1 and b_2 are regression coefficients obtained from the auxiliary regression of the match parameter associated with a job (ϕ) on total work experience and on tenure, and where $\gamma_{X_0 T}$ is the least squares regression of tenure on initial work experience. Previous arguments imply that if there is systematic job changing $b_1 > 0$ and $b_1 + b_2 > 0$. More importantly, systematic job changing implies that better jobs will be found later in the working life and so will be associated with longer tenure, $\gamma_{X_0 T} > 0$. Thus, the estimated tenure effect will be downward biased, and total experience effects upward biased. Estimates of the tenure effect on wages using the two-step procedure will therefore establish a lower bound on the true tenure effect.

Applying this estimation strategy to data from the Panel Survey of Income Dynamics, Topel finds that the effect of an additional year of tenure on wages is non-negligible. The first year of tenure increases wages by about 5.5 percent, which is almost as large as the effect of the first year of total work experience. That is, if an individual left a job exogenously after having worked only one year on the job, a new job would, on average, have a wage that is lower than the old job by the above tenure effect. The new job would, however, have a wage that is on average higher by 7 percent (the total experience return) than that of a new entrant.

4.2.2 Wolpin's Structural Turnover Model

As noted, another approach is to model the behavioral decision process underlying mobility decisions concretely, embedding in the model different structural fundamentals that can potentially be responsible for the observed positive tenure-wage relationship. A fairly simple model was outlined above. Wolpin (1992) provides a concrete illustration of the potential value of this approach.[58] It is useful to present the structure of the model.

In that paper an individual's career profile is characterized as consisting of L cycles, each beginning with an unemployment period followed by a series of consecutive jobs with different employers. For the 1th cycle,

$$c_l = \left(d_l, e_{l1}, e_{l2}, ..., e_{ls_l} \right),\qquad(56)$$

where d_l is the length of the unemployment spell that begins the 1th cycle, e_{l1} is the length of the first job spell in cycle 1, e_{l2} the length of the second job spell in cycle 1, etc. New cycles begin whenever there is a transition from a job to unemployment, so that all employment spells within a cycle are contiguous. The lifetime career profile is

$$c = \left(c_1, c_2, ..., c_L \right).\qquad(57)$$

Job or occupation changes within an employment spell with the same employer are ignored, but employment spells with the same employer that are separated by an employment spell with another employer or by an unemployment spell are tracked. Thus, for example, the first employment spell after a period of unemployment will be the last employer of the previous spell if the individual was laid off and recalled.

The model provides a discrete time characterization of the lifetime career as depicted in (56) and (57). The individual is assumed to have a linear additive per-period utility function (in the wage and in the value of leisure or non-market production (b)) and to face a number of constraints imposed by the labor market environment. These environmental constraints are:

(1) In each period of quit-unemployment, that is, unemployment that begins with a quit, there is a known probability of receiving a wage offer, P_1, that may be history dependent. Offers are never received from previous employers after quits.

(2) In each period of layoff-unemployment, there is a known probability of receiving an offer from the previous employer, i.e. a recall offer, P_4.

(3) In each period of employment, there is a known probability of receiving a wage offer, P_2, from another employer that may be history dependent.

(4) In each period of employment, there is a known probability of layoff, P_3, that may be history dependent.

(5) There is a fixed and known unemployment insurance benefit (c) paid for a fixed duration (n^*) of any layoff-unemployment spell.

(6) Wage offers (w) depend on the number of periods worked (total or general experience, GK) and on the number of periods worked at the current employer (specific experience or tenure, SK). There is an employer- or match-specific component of the wage that is part of the wage offer (u) and that is drawn from a known distribution; once an offer is accepted there is no further stochastic wage variation on that job.

The expected discounted lifetime utility at any time (age) differs according to the current employment state and the career history, which is summarized by GK, SK and n (the length of the current unemployment spell). Obviously, there are restrictions on the set of feasible histories at any time. For example, $GK + n$ at time t must be less than $t - 1$ and SK cannot be larger than GK. Individuals choose the action, conditional on feasibility, at every age that maximizes their expected present discounted value of utility. Letting V_t^Q be the expected lifetime utility at period t given the individual is currently unemployed via a quit, V_t^L the expected lifetime utility if on layoff at t and V_t^E the expected lifetime utility if employed at t, their Bellman (1957) value function representations are (for $t < T$):

$$V_t^Q(n, Gk) = b + \beta\left\{P_1(n+1, GK)E_t\left[\max\left(V_t^Q(n+1, GK), V_{t+1}^E(u, 0, GK)\right)\right]\right.$$
$$\left. + (1 - P_1(n+1, GK))V_{t+1}^Q(n+1, GK)\right\},$$

$$V_t^L(n, SK, GK) = b + c(n) + \beta\left\{P_1(n+1, GK)E_t\left[\max\left(V_{t+1}^L(n+1, SK, GK), V_{t+1}^E(u, 0, GK)\right)\right]\right.$$
$$+ P_4(n+1, SK)E_t\left[\max\left(V_{t+1}^L(n+1, SK, GK), V_{t+1}^E(u, SK, GK)\right)\right]$$
$$\left. + (1 - P_1(n+1, GK) - P_4(n+1, SK)V_{t+1}^L(n+1, SK, GK)\right\},$$

$$V_t^E(u, SK, GK) = w_t(SK, GK, u) + \beta\left\{P_2(GK+1)E_t\left[\max\left(V_{t+1}^Q(0, GK+1), V_{t+1}^E(u', 0, GK+1)\right)\right]\right.$$
$$\left. + (1 - P_2(GK+1))V_{t+1}^Q(0, GK+1)\right\} \quad if \quad u < u_{t+1}^{*Q}(0, SK+1, GK+1),$$

$$V_t^E(u, SK, GK) = w_t(SK, GK, u)$$
$$+ \beta\left\{P_2(GK+1)(1 - P_3(SK+1))E_t\left[\max\left(V_{t+1}^E(u, SK+1, GK+1), V_{t+1}^E(u', 0, GK+1)\right)\right]\right.$$
$$+ P_2(GK+1)P_3(SK+1)E_t\left[\max\left(V_{t+1}^L(0, SK+1, GK+1), V_{t+1}^E(u', 0, GK+1)\right)\right]$$
$$+ (1 - P_2(GK+1))P_3(SK+1)V_{t+1}^L(0, SK+1, GK+1)$$
$$\left. + (1 - P_2(GK+1))(1 - P_3(SK+1))V_{t+1}^E(u, SK+1, GK+1)\right\}$$
$$if \quad u > u_{t+1}^*Q(0, SK+1, GK+1). \tag{58}$$

The terminal period value functions are b, $b + c(n)$ and $w_T(SK, GK, u)$, respectively.

The value at time t of having quit into unemployment n periods ago with *GK* periods of prior work experience consists of the value of leisure obtained in that period plus the discounted value of the expected maximal utility obtained if a job offer is received and either rejected (in which case the individual remains in the quit state with an extra period of unemployment and no further work experience) or accepted (in which case the individual receives the value of being employed at a new employer, i.e. with no specific experience, with the preceding period's general work experience, and with a new wage draw, u) times the probability of receiving an offer plus the discounted value of remaining in the quit state with an additional period of unemployment times the probability that a job offer is not received. Note that the value of being in the quit state depends on history only because the offer probability is assumed to directly depend on the unemployment spell duration and on general work experience. Similarly, the value of being in the layoff state is the value of leisure plus unemployment compensation benefits if still eligible, plus the appropriately discounted expected utility if an offer is received from a new firm or if a recall offer is received. It is assumed that a recall offer and an offer from a new firm cannot both be received in the same period.

The existence of a 'quit-into-unemployment' value function implicitly assumes that such a choice can potentially be optimal. Recall that there are no new wage draws on a job after the first period of employment on that job (although wages will grow deterministically with job experience) and that the value of leisure is not random, so quitting into unemployment can not arise because the current value of leisure increases relative to the wage at the current employer. To see how quit behavior could arise, it is instructive to consider a two period model. Suppose that an individual is now in period two having accepted a job in period one with a particular u. Then the individual would quit into unemployment in period two only if $b > w$ $(1, 1, u)$. However, in order to have accepted the job in period one it must have been true that

$$w(0,0,u) + \beta\left\{P_2(1)E\left[\max\left(b, w(0,1,u')\right)\right] + \left(1 - P_2(1)\right)b\right\}$$
$$> b + \beta\left\{P_1(1,0)E\left[\max\left(b, w(0,0,u')\right)\right] + \left(1 - P_1(1,0)\right)b\right\}, \qquad (59)$$

where the condition for quitting into unemployment has been assumed in the derivation of (59) and where layoffs have been ignored for convenience. Now, b must be greater than $w(0, 0, u)$ (since it is greater than $w(1, 1, u)$, and

$w(0,0,u')$ cannot be larger than $w(0,1,u')$. Thus, quits into unemployment may arise if either the probability of receiving an offer from a new employer while currently employed ($P_2(1)$) is sufficiently larger than the probability of receiving an offer while unemployed ($P_1(1, 0)$) or there is sufficiently large wage return to general experience, or a combination of both. The intuition for this behavior is that a job in this model is an investment good both because of the accumulation of general capital and because employment generates new offers, and the value of the investment good increases with the distance from the horizon. There will thus exist a range of u values for which the job will be accepted in period one with full knowledge that if a 'better' job doesn't come along the individual will quit into unemployment the next period.

Obviously, the finite horizon is essential for this result. Further, the result generalizes to any finite-period model; indeed, in the multiperiod setting, individuals may accept an offer in some period knowing that they will quit into unemployment some finite number of periods in the future. Thus, this result has the flavor of there being a tryout period even though there is no explicit learning in the model.

It is because of this behavior that the value function for the employment state in (58) has a two-part representation depending on whether there will be a voluntary quit into unemployment in the subsequent period. If a quit will be optimal, then the quit value function is the relevant comparison to the value of receiving an offer from a new firm, while if a quit will not be optimal, then the value of remaining with the current employer is the relevant comparison to a new offer.[59]

The current wage draw, u, is the only randomness in the model. Decision rules are thus described fully and uniquely by a set of state- and time-dependent reservation values for u, which are implicitly defined as follows:

$$V_t^Q(n, GK) = V_t^E\left(u_t^{*Q}(n, SK, GK), SK, GK\right),$$

$$V_t^L(n, SK, GK) = V_t^E\left(u_t^{*L}(n, SK, GK), 0, GK\right),$$

$$V_t^L(n, SK, GK) = V_t^E\left(u_t^{*R}(n, SK, GK), SK, GK\right),$$

$$V_t^E(u, SK, GK) = V_t^E\left(u_t^{*N}(u, SK, GK), 0, GK\right). \tag{60}$$

The first reservation value, u_t^{*Q}, defines the value of u at which the individual is indifferent between employment and unemployment — if the individual is currently unemployed having quit sometime in the past ($n > 0$, $SK = 0$), then it defines the value of u necessary to induce the individual to accept an offer, while if the individual is currently employed ($n = 0$, $SK > 0$), then it defines the value of u necessary to induce the individual to remain with the firm rather than quitting into unemployment. The second reservation value, u_t^{*L}, is the value of u at which an individual will just accept an offer from a new firm while on layoff. This reservation value differs from that value of u necessary to induce the individual to return to the old employer if recalled from a layoff, u_t^{*R}. Finally, u_t^{*N} is the value of u at which an individual will be induced to leave the current firm for a new employer.

An interesting feature of the model is that it can readily explain declining unemployment hazards without having to appeal to duration dependent offer probabilities, as was done in Wolpin (1987). The reason is closely related to the existence of quit-unemployment. If, for example, offer probabilities are larger when employed than when unemployed, then the value of employment will fall with the duration of unemployment relative to that of remaining unemployed. Thus, the wage draw necessary to induce exit from unemployment will be increasing. As the offer probabilities are specified, the model is flexible enough to accommodate even non-monotonic hazards.

The sequences of reservation values given in (60) completely describe the solution to the individual's optimization problem. Given that analytical solutions cannot be obtained, it is necessary to develop a numerical algorithm to solve for the reservation wage sequences. As in any standard finite-horizon dynamic programming problem, the solution can be obtained recursively beginning at T. However, owing to the structure of the model, a number of approximations were required for tractability. The details are provided in Appendix A. The major simplifications were: (1) The random component of the wage, a continuous state variable, was discretized. The discretization of u was taken to be a discrete approximation of a normal variate, with the wage offer function assumed to be of the form $w(SK,GK)e^u$. The integrations necessary to calculate the value functions in (58) were performed also with this discretization; (2) To reduce the effective size of the state space, the individual was assumed to optimize quarterly (the length of a period in the data) only over the first 24 quarters. The calculation of future value functions after that length of time was carried out over annual decision periods for 12 years, and then over 10 biannual periods — the total horizon was 38 years.

The parameters of the model were estimated by maximum likelihood. The reservation u's determined as the solution of the dynamic programming problem serve as the input to the likelihood function. The likelihood function is the product over the sample observations of the probabilities associated with particular career profiles, i.e.

$$
\begin{aligned}
L &= \prod_{i=1}^{I} Pr(c_i) \\
&= \prod_{i=1}^{I} Pr\left(d_1, e^1, d_2, e^2, \ldots, d_L, e^L\right) \\
&= \prod_{i=1}^{I} Pr(d_1) Pr(e^1) \ldots Pr(d_L) Pr(e^L).
\end{aligned}
\tag{61}
$$

Recall that career profiles are represented by a spell of unemployment followed by consecutive employment spells, where the e's are vectors of employment spells within each of the L cycles. The third line in (61) is a consequence of the assumption that the new job wage draws are independent. Employment spells within cycles are not independent because the acceptance wage draw on one job depends on the wage draw of the previous job, that is, u^{*N} as seen in (60) directly depends on u.[60] Thus, the likelihood function requires multivariate integrations of order given by the number of consecutive separate employer spells in a cycle. The details of the likelihood function are provided in Appendix B.

The data used in the analysis are from the NLSY and consist of a subsample of men who graduated from high school, primarily between 1978 and 1982, and who never attended college (at least through 1985). The reader is referred to the original paper for details. Table 5 presents selected characteristics of employment profiles at each of the first twenty calendar quarters after having graduated. Although the race differences are interesting and were in fact the focus of the original paper, the interest here is in showing the evolution of employment experiences and so the discussion will generally focus on overall patterns.

Consider first the character of unemployment.[61] The majority of high school graduates have an initial spell of unemployment upon graduation, although it is surprising how many transit immediately to a full time job.[62] The fraction of the population unemployed declines steadily, but is still reasonably high even four years after graduation. Decomposing unemployment by whether it was initiated as a quit or as a layoff (the remainder is the first unemployment spell directly upon leaving school, which is neither a quit nor a layoff), the proportion unemployed having quit a job sometime in

TABLE 5
Quarterly State Variables for the Estimation Sample by Race

| QUARTER | SAMPLE SIZE | | FRACTION UNEMPLOYED | | | | | | AVERAGE GENERAL EXPERIENCE* | | AVERAGE SPECIFIC EXPERIENCE* | | AVERAGE CURRENT DURATION OF UNEMPLOYMENT* | | AVERAGE WAGE† | |
| | | | Total | | Quit | | Layoff | | | | | | | | | |
	Black	White	Black	White	Black	White	Black	White	Black	White	Black	White	Black	White	Black	White
1	322	543	.717	.532	.000	.000	.000	.000	.283	.468	.283	.468	.717	.532	2,713	3,077
2	312	527	.654	.464	.010	.017	.042	.033	.612	.998	.583	.941	1.26	.861	2,823	2,994
3	296	491	.661	.450	.017	.041	.071	.063	.953	1.51	.895	1.35	1.71	1.19	2,750	3,115
4	283	473	.572	.395	.042	.061	.078	.057	1.34	2.09	1.19	1.79	2.03	1.33	2,699	3,166
5	277	456	.520	.375	.036	.061	.090	.075	1.80	2.69	1.55	2.28	2.22	1.50	2,747	3,224
6	254	431	.508	.339	.066	.056	.103	.084	2.24	3.32	1.85	2.77	2.48	1.56	2,677	3,283
7	242	403	.537	.372	.050	.066	.136	.109	2.70	3.92	2.24	3.15	2.88	1.78	2,810	3,364
8	230	365	.478	.318	.057	.069	.122	.090	3.25	4.52	2.63	3.65	2.98	1.72	2,913	3,385
9	225	341	.458	.290	.062	.065	.107	.082	3.78	5.13	2.95	4.08	3.25	1.72	2,945	3,376
10	214	319	.435	.285	.061	.063	.103	.085	4.33	5.85	3.35	4.58	3.41	1.87	2,941	3,352
11	187	287	.455	.286	.070	.080	.112	.094	4.81	6.56	3.56	4.99	3.78	1.83	2,972	3,477
12	178	261	.393	.245	.073	.088	.067	.063	5.39	7.32	3.98	5.40	3.06	1.64	2,871	3,525
13	174	246	.333	.207	.069	.059	.034	.065	6.09	8.13	4.20	5.87	3.47	1.51	2,920	3,525
14	165	237	.352	.194	.061	.065	.061	.076	6.70	8.94	4.58	6.49	3.68	1.32	3,019	3,530
15	122	197	.361	.203	.057	.051	.074	.096	7.35	9.90	5.15	7.31	4.03	1.46	3,165	3,697
16	109	173	.294	.173	.037	.035	.064	.087	8.38	11.0	6.03	8.09	3.55	1.34	3,254	3,673
17	104	163	.269	.110	.038	.031	.058	.043	9.24	11.8	6.33	8.98	3.44	.96	3,230	3,690
18	95	149	.221	.107	.021	.034	.042	.034	10.3	12.9	7.11	9.89	3.26	.99	3,254	3,648
19	72	117	.264	.068	.041	.017	.055	.026	11.0*	14.2	7.82	10.8	3.71	.59	3,228	3,795
20	62	106	.145	.047	.000	.009	.000	.009	11.9	15.1	7.09	11.6	2.90	.58	3,135	3,929

* Values are based on end-of-quarter distributions.

† Sample sizes are smaller because of both nonemployment and missing data.

Source: Wolpin, K. I. (1992): The Determinants of Black-White Differences in Early Employment Careers: Search, Layoffs, Quits, and Endogenous Wage Growth. *Journal of Political Economy*, **100**.

the past is somewhat smaller than the proportion unemployed as a result of a past layoff. Quit-unemployment reaches a peak of almost nine percent in the white population while layoff unemployment reaches a peak of almost 11 percent.

General work experience accumulates slowly at first and then more rapidly as more and more of the population transits to steady employment. Specific work experience accumulates less rapidly as general experience is acquired in part through job turnover. The real wage path is consistent with the growth in skills that would accompany the accumulation of work experience.

Before turning to the estimates of the wage-tenure effect, it is useful to highlight some of the other findings. Within the context of this single framework, one is able to address a set of connected questions that have generally been posed in isolation. They include: What are the effects of unemployment insurance on the length of unemployment spells, the accumulation of work experience, and on wages? Is the probability of receiving job offers while unemployed greater or smaller than the probability while employed and how are they affected by employment histories? To what extent is a layoff a binding constraint as opposed to (recall) offers that workers reject? What is the relationship of layoff and recall rates to employment histories? What is the effect of general work experience and of employer-specific work experience on wages?

Unemployed job offer rates

The probability of receiving a job offer in the first period after high school graduation ($n = 0$, $GK = 0$) is estimated to be .55 for whites and .65 for blacks. For neither group is the offer probability very sensitive to the duration of the spell of unemployment. With 20 quarters of work experience (and $n = 0$), the offer probability is .38 for whites and .83 for blacks. These estimates are somewhat higher (on a weekly basis) than those that have been obtained only from unemployment spell data.

Employed job offer rates

The probability of receiving a job offer while employed is .60 for blacks and .24 for whites. After 20 quarters of work experience the probabilities are .45 and .26.

Layoff rates

Layoff rates are .06 for blacks and .05 for whites in the first quarter of their employment. The rate falls to .05 and .03, respectively, after 20 quarters of specific experience.

Recall rates

Regardless of race, tenure or layoff duration, the probability of receiving a recall offer conditional on not receiving an offer from a new employer is almost unity. The reason for having a layoff spell beyond a single quarter is the (possibly implicit) rejection of recall offers.

Wage offers, tenure, and experience

The annual percentage increase in the real wage (offer) due to an additional year of general experience (after having obtained five years of general experience), holding specific experience constant, is about 2 percent for blacks and 7.5 percent for whites. With respect to tenure, the first year of specific experience, holding general experience constant, increases the real wage (offer) by about 7 percent for blacks and 5 percent for whites. These estimates are very close to the estimate obtained by Topel as a lower bound. Interestingly, the variance in wage offers is considerably larger for whites than for blacks, which contributes to faster wage growth among whites.

It is somewhat comforting in terms of the credibility of the structural estimation exercise that Wolpin's estimate of the tenure effect on wages is similar to the estimate obtained from Topel's more robust procedure. The gains from estimating the structural model are considerable in terms of the information it provides about parameters of interest and the kinds of policy experiments that can be performed. However, the structural model assumes that all of the relationships are fundamental, when they are clearly not. As discussed in the context of the simple two-state search model, offer probabilities are likely to be behaviorally determined. Moreover, layoff rates would be sensitive to the level of unemployment compensation benefits (Topel (1984)). Therefore, *ceteris paribus* policy experiments can be misleading. But, this is merely to say that there is considerable scope for further work.

5. A GENERAL FRAMEWORK FOR ESTIMABLE MODELS OF LABOR FORCE DYNAMICS

Behaviorally based models of labor force dynamics can be characterized generally within a discrete choice dynamic programming framework (DDP).

Such DDP models have been receiving increasing attention over the last decade, with applications to industrial organization, economic demography, development economics, public finance, health economics, as well as labor economics. Although there have been several recent surveys of that literature, e.g. Eckstein and Wolpin (1989) and Rust (forthcoming), it is useful to show the connection explicitly.

Consider a general model in which an individual decides among (at most) K possible alternatives in each of T (finite) discrete periods of time. Alternatives are defined to be mutually exclusive so that if $d_k(t) = 1$ indicates that alternative k is chosen at time t and $d_k(t) = 0$ indicates otherwise, then $\sum_{k=1}^{K} d_k(t) = 1$. Associated with each choice at time t is a current period reward, $R_k(t)$, that is known to the individual at time t but that is random from the perspective of periods prior to t.

The objective of the individual at any time $t = 0, ..., T$, is to maximize

$$E\left[\sum_{\tau=t}^{T} \beta^{\tau-t} \sum_{k \in K} R_k(\tau) d_k(\tau) \,\middle|\, S(t) \right], \tag{62}$$

where $\beta > 0$ is the individual's discount factor, $E(\cdot)$ is the mathematical expectations operator, and $S(t)$ is the state space at time t. The state space consists of all factors, known to the individual, that affect current rewards or the probability distribution of any of the future rewards.

Maximization of (62) is accomplished by choice of the optimal sequence of control variables $\{d_k(t)\}_{k \in K}$ for $t = 0, ..., T$. Define the maximal expected value of the discounted lifetime reward at t as

$$V(S(t), t) = \max_{\{d_k(t)\}_{k \in K}} E\left[\sum_{\tau=t}^{T} \beta^{\tau-t} \sum_{k=1}^{K} R_k(\tau) d_k(\tau) \,\middle|\, S(t) \right]. \tag{63}$$

The value function $V(S(t), t)$, depends on the state space at t and on t itself (due to the finiteness of the horizon or the direct effect of age on rewards), and can be written as

$$V(S(t), t) = \max_{k \in K} \left\{ V_k(S(t), t) \right\}, \tag{64}$$

where $V_k(S(t), t)$, the alternative-specific expected lifetime reward or value function, obeys the Bellman equation (Bellman, 1957)

$$V_k\big(S(t),t\big)= R_k\big(S(t),t\big)+ \beta E\big[V\big(S(t+1),t+1\big)\big|\,S(t),d_k(t)=1\big], \quad t \le T-1,$$

$$V_k\big(S(T),T\big)= R_k\big(S(T),T\big). \tag{65}$$

Notice that the dependence of the current period reward on the state space (or at least a subset of it) is made explicit in (65). As seen in (65), the alternative-specific value function assumes that future choices are optimally made for any given current period decision. The expectation in (65) is taken over the distribution of $S(t+1)$ conditional on $S(t)$ and $d_k(t) = 1$, with the conditional density denoted by

$$p_{kt}\big(S(t+1)\big|\,S(t),d_k(t)=1\big). \tag{66}$$

The randomness in rewards arises from the existence of state variables at time $t+1$ observable to the agent at $t+1$, but unobservable at t or before. The formulation in (66) allows for contemporaneously and serially correlated rewards.

To make explicit the connection of the above framework to models of labor force dynamics, consider the simplest two-state job search model. Let $k = 1$ indicate search and $k = 2$ work. Then, the reward functions are simply $R_1(t) = -c$ and $R_2(t) = w_t$, where c is the search cost and w is the wage offer. The only state variable is the current wage offer which evolves (as in (66)) according to $p_{1t}\big(w_{t+1}\big|\,w_t,d_1(t)=1\big)= dF(w)$ and $p_{2t}\big(w_{t+1}\big|\,w_t,d_2(t)=1\big)= w_t$, where F is the distribution function of wage offers (offers are serially independent). The value function (64) is the maximum over the alternative specific value functions, which correspond to equation (65). Adopting the terminal value function condition in (65) closes the model. Specifications with more complicated structures can be similarly represented. The key to that representation is that the value function (64) is specified over mutually exclusive choices; thus, in Wolpin's turnover model, there are several sets of value functions depending on whether or not the individual is currently unemployed due to a quit and has received a job offer, unemployed due to a layoff with a recall offer, unemployed due to a layoff with an offer from a new employer, or employed with an offer from another employer (see equation (58)).

As is clear from the discussion of the turnover model, a major limiting factor in the empirical implementation of DDP models is their computational complexity. The inherent computational problem of this approach has been accommodated in the literature in several ways. In many applications the dimensionality of the problem, both in terms of the number of choices and the size of the state space, has been kept small. A significant part of the literature has been restricted to problems of only two alternatives. Among the earliest contributions of this type were studies of the following dichotomous decisions: to re-enlist in the air force or not (Gotz and McCall, 1984), to remain in an occupation or choose a different occupation (Miller, 1984), to renew a patent or let it expire (Pakes, 1987), to replace a bus engine or not (Rust, 1987), to have a child or not (Wolpin, 1984).

A number of alternatives to reducing the size of the choice set and/or the state space have been developed and implemented. They can be classified as methods that rely on the full solution of the dynamic programming model but take advantage of particular structures, functional forms or distributional assumptions (Miller, 1984; Pakes, 1987; Rust, 1987), or methods that circumvent having to solve completely the optimization problem (Hotz and Miller, 1993; Manski, 1991; Hotz, Miller, Sanders and Smith, 1994). Notice that there are no conceptual problems in implementing models with large choice sets, large state spaces, and serial dependencies in unobservables. The problem is in implementing interesting economic models that are computationally tractable.

Computational simplifications for handling large choice sets and/or large state spaces (which includes the case of serially correlated unobservables), while remaining within a full-solution paradigm, have involved finding convenient forms for the reward functions and error distributions.[63] Miller (1984), Pakes (1987), and Rust (1987) are the leading examples of this approach. The approach in Rust has been more widely adopted in the economics literature, perhaps because of its structural similarity with the static random utility model.[64] That formulation has also served as the basis for the implementation of several of the non-full solution methods discussed below.

Rust makes the following assumptions: (i) the reward functions are additively separable in the unobservables, with each unobservable associated with a mutually exclusive choice, (ii) the unobservables are conditionally independent, i.e. conditional on observable state variables, the unobservables are serially independent, and (iii) the unobservables are distributed as multivariate extreme value. There are two very appealing consequences of these assumptions for solution and estimation:

1. The $Emax(\cdot)$ function, the expectations functions appearing in (65), has the closed form solution

$$E\left[V(S(t),t)\right] = \gamma + \tau \, \ln\left\{\sum_{k=1}^{K} \frac{\exp\left(\overline{V}_k\left(\overline{S}(t),t\right)\right)}{\tau}\right\}, \tag{67}$$

where $\overline{V}_k$ is the expectation of the alternative-specific value functions, the expectation of (65), and γ is Euler's constant. Thus, multivariate numerical integrations are avoided in solving the dynamic programming problem. It should be noted that (conditional) independence of the alternative-specific errors is not sufficient to obtain an analytical form; additive separability and the extreme value assumptions are crucial.

2. The choice probabilities are multinomial logit, i.e. with τ normalized to unity,

$$Pr\left(d_k(t) = 1\right) \big| \overline{S}(t) = \frac{\exp\left(\overline{V}_k\left(\overline{S}(t),t\right)\right)}{\displaystyle\sum_{j \in K} \exp\left(V_j\left(S(t),t\right)\right)}. \tag{68}$$

Therefore, multivariate numerical integrations are also avoided in likelihood estimation. However, as in the static logit model, only limited forms of correlation among the alternative-specific errors can be accommodated.[65]

In addition to simplifications achieved through functional form assumptions, there are several examples in the published literature of what can be viewed as a simplification achieved through an approximation to the full solution. The paper by Wolpin (1992) discussed in detail above is one example. Stock and Wise (1990) estimate a model of retirement which they call an 'option value' model, but which is equivalent to substituting the maximum of the expected alternative-specific value functions for the expected maximum of the alternative-specific value functions. Lumsdaine, Stock, and Wise (1992) evaluated the performance of this approximation vs. the exact solution in predicting the effect of the pension window plan studied by Stock and Wise, and concluded that the fit was about the same. Stern (1991), analyzing a different model of retirement concluded from simulation evidence that while the approximation did predict well the large impact of a pension window, it did not predict well other dynamic aspects of the model.

More recently, Keane and Wolpin (1994) have developed an approximation method that consists of simulating the multiple integrations required in the full solution by Monte Carlo integration for a subset of the state space elements and interpolating the non-simulated values using a specific regression function. They obtain Monte Carlo evidence that shows that the overall performance of the method is excellent and have applied the method (Keane and Wolpin, 1994) to a model of schooling and occupational choice. As an alternative to approximating value functions, Geweke, Slonim and Zarkin (1992) have proposed a solution and estimation method based on approximating the agent's decision rules that still recovers structural parameters.

The non-full-solution methods that have appeared in the literature, Hotz and Miller (1993), Hotz, Miller, Sanders and Smith (1994), and Manski (1988), use alternative representations of the future component of the choice-specific valuations that do not depend explicitly on the structural parameters of the model. The $Emax(\cdot)$ functions are estimated from data on future choice or reward probabilities. Because the choice-specific valuation functions are specified in the first two papers as they are presented above, it is relatively easy to describe their methodologies. However, the representation in Manski's path utility framework is sufficiently different that we will forgo discussion of it. Manski's approach does share many of the same advantages and drawbacks.[66]

The insight of Hotz and Miller can be most easily illustrated under Rust's assumptions. Using (67) and (68), it can be shown that

$$
E\left[V\big(S(t),t\big)\right] = \sum_{k=1}^{K} Pr\Big(d_k(t)=1 \,\Big|\, \overline{S}(t)\Big) \times
$$
$$
\left[\gamma + \overline{V}_k\big(\overline{S}(t),t\big) - \ln\Big(Pr\big(d_k(t)=1 \,\big|\, \overline{S}(t)\big)\Big)\right]. \quad (69)
$$

Successive forward substitution for $\overline{V}_k\big(\overline{S}(t),t\big)$, recognizing that it contains future expected maximum functions, implies that the expected maximum function at any t can be written as a function of the future conditional choice probabilities. Hotz and Miller show that this result is not dependent on the extreme value distribution assumption, but generalizes to any distribution. The extreme value distribution is appealing because the representation has a closed form. Empirical implementation uses data on observed future choices to obtain the conditional choice probabilities that are needed for calculating alternative-specific value functions. Because choice probabilities are obtained non-parametrically from the data and are state-specific, implementation may require very large observation sets, particularly when the state space is large. Structural parameters are recovered from the contemporaneous reward functions, which are the only places they enter in this formulation. The estimation therefore does not take into account all of the parameter restrictions contained in the theory.

Although this method is significantly more tractable than a full solution method, an inherent limitation of this approach is that it cannot admit to the existence of individual-specific unobservables as a component of the state space, generally ruling out forms of serial correlation including permanent unobserved heterogeneity. Furthermore the $Emax(\cdot)$ values calculated from the data are obviously not policy invariant as they depend on the structural parameters of the model. Thus, full solution would be necessary after estimation in order to conduct policy experiments.

The methodology in Hotz, Miller, Sanders, and Smith also uses the Hotz and Miller representation theorem. However, rather than computing the alternative-specific valuation functions by considering all feasible future paths as in Hotz and Miller, they simulate future paths in calculating the expected maximum functions, using (67) in the extreme value case. Noting that in the extreme value case, for example, the expected values of the alternative-specific value functions (normalized against one of the alternatives) are just the log-odds of the choice probabilities, data on choice probabilities are sufficient to estimate (non-parametrically) the normalized value functions. Parameter estimates are obtained by comparing the data to the simulated value functions using a weighted distance estimator. Because the estimator is linear in the simulated value functions, analogous to the MSM estimator, only one future path needs to be simulated to obtain consistent estimates. While this method is even more tractable computationally than Hotz and Miller, its limitations are not different.

6. CONCLUDING REMARKS

The empirical literature on labor force dynamics has made enormous progress over the last twenty years. Regardless of their limitations, the initial pioneering attempts simply to relate unemployment duration data to observable characteristics with economic theory in mind were critical to that progress. Statistical advances in the use of duration data have led to a revolution in the empirical implementation of the reduced form approach to the study of labor force dynamics. Finally, the development of methods to estimate structural parameters of dynamic discrete choice models has begun what in my view will be another revolution in the way, as stated in the Econometric Society's constitution, 'the unification of theoretical and factual studies in economics' is achieved. There are few empirical literatures in economics that have been as successful.

However, there is still much to be done. We know far too little to make confident policy statements. Significant progress will require that we take a more active role in the collection of data. The fact is that almost none of the variables that are used in the analysis of labor market transition decisions are collected with the intention of matching them to the parameters of the behavioral models that underlie the empirical work and the effect of using proxies is unknown. In addition, comparisons between alternative empirical methodologies must continue to be made to determine the relative merits of structural and reduced form estimation. Finally, the estimation of equilibrium models, currently in its infancy, should continue to be pursued as the best long run strategy for policy analysis.

NOTES

1. For example, Atkinson and Mickelwright (1992) survey the literature on unemployment insurance effects, while Mortensen (1986) surveys a substantial part of the theoretical literature on labor dynamics.
2. See for example Kiefer (1988) or Lancaster (1990).
3. An alternative behavioral assumption is that the individual drops out of the labor force upon reaching the end of the horizon. In either case, the idea is that the individual has only a fixed amount of resources available to search. Which assumption is adopted may depend on the sample one is considering. More importantly, one would probably wish to embed the single spell two-state model in a more complete model in which future spells of unemployment have positive probability and the accumulation of such resources is part of an optimal strategy. There is an implicit assumption in the formulation in the text that the individual always has enough resources to wait for the arrival of an offer once the terminal period is reached. A formal model of job search with borrowing constraints has not been empirically implemented in the literature.
4. For the treatment of that case the reader is referred to Eckstein and Wolpin (1989).
5. With a positive exogenous layoff probability, λ, in the infinite horizon case $1 - \lambda$ multiplies the discount factor. Allowing for exogenous separations is more complicated in the finite horizon case because of the non-stationarity in reservation wages.
6. The continuous time analogue to (4) and (5) are developed in Flinn and Heckman (1982a) and in Mortensen (1986). In the finite horizon case the difference equation is replaced by a

differential equation, which can be solved numerically by taking a discrete-time approximation over small intervals (see Van den Berg, 1990). In both infinite and finite horizon cases, the offer probability is replaced by a Poisson parameter.

7. van den Berg (1990) provides analogous comparative dynamic predictions for the continuous time finite horizon model in which the fundamental parameters are themselves continuously time-varying.

8. The result is easily demonstrated using an induction argument applied to equation (4).

9. For example, an increase in the probability of receiving an offer, because it increases the reservation wage, may either increase or decrease the hazard rate and lengthen unemployment durations. van den Berg (1991) has recently shown the conditions for the hazard rate to decline as the offer probability increases are fairly weak and are satisfied by most distributions generally used in job search models.

10. An exception is the data from the Netherlands used by van den Berg (1990) that includes respondent perceptions about the lowest and highest wage believed to be obtainable.

11. A full-time job is one which satisfies two conditions: (1) it must have lasted a full calendar quarter and; (2) hours worked must have been at least 30 in each of the 13 weeks. This definition, then, does not correspond exactly to continuous unemployment.

12. Classen (1977), Burgess and Kingston (1977), and Kahn (1978) report similar evidence.

13. The situation is more complicated if one drops the assumption that jobs last forever, that is, that unemployment may be a recurring state and that eligibility for unemployment compensation depends on prior employment. See Mortensen (1977) or the recent survey of the unemployment insurance literature by Atkinson and Micklewright (1992),

14. In the discrete time case, the proof that expected duration is the inverse of the hazard rate requires showing that

$$h \sum_{n=0}^{\infty} n(1-h)^n = \frac{1}{h}$$

Using the fact that $\sum_{n=0}^{\infty} \frac{a_n x^n}{1-x} = \sum_{n=0}^{\infty} (a_0 + a_1 + \ldots + a_n) x^n$ and setting $a_j = 1$ for all j and $x = 1 - h$, one gets the required result. To prove the proposition in the continuous time case, note that when the hazard rate is independent of duration, the (continuous) density function for duration must be exponential, i.e., $f(d) = he^{-hd}$.

15. $E(\ln d) = \sum_{d=0}^{\infty} \ln d \, f_d$. In the continuous time case with constant hazard, it can be demonstrated that

$$E(\ln d) = -\ln h + \psi(1)$$

where $\psi(1)$ is a known constant. See Lancaster (1990).

16. Other examples are Burgess and Kingston (1977), Classen (1977), Kahn (1978), and Newton and Rosen (1979).

17. Actually they write the second equation as the log of the ratio of the accepted wage to the pre-unemployment wage, but they include the log of the pre-unemployment wage as a regressor.

18. The discussion that follows is not specifically related to the Ehrenberg–Oaxaca paper, but represents a composite of explanations for the replacement rate specification.

19. Another reason sometimes cited is that the pre-unemployment wage measures the opportunity cost of remaining unemployed. Such an interpretation is not consistent with the search model; the opportunity cost is the value of search given by (2).

20. It is straightforward to show that

$$\frac{\sigma_\omega^2 \, \sigma_{\pi,\mu}^2}{\sigma_B^2 \, \sigma_{w^r,}^2 - \left(\sigma_{B,w^r,}\right)^2} < \frac{\sigma_{\pi,\mu}^2}{\sigma_B^2}$$

is equivalent to

$$\sigma_B^2 \, \sigma_{\pi,\mu}^2 - \left(\sigma_{B,\pi,\mu}\right)^2 > 0$$

which must always be true.

21. The existence of cross-equation restrictions is obviously not dependent on the Pareto assumption.

22. The common ratio is $-1/\alpha +1$.

23. Among such studies are those by Kasper (1967) and Feldstein and Poterba (1984). For further references, see Devine and Kiefer (1991).

24. Assume that the reservation wage contains reporting error.

25. It should be noted that the comparative static expression that is relied on above to estimate $\dfrac{\partial w^*}{\partial \mu}$ does not apply in the finite horizon case, and thus, their estimate of the duration effect on the reservation wage is not consistent in specifications of the reservation wage that include duration.

26. See Kalbfleish and Prentice (1980).

27. See Kalbfleish and Prentice (1980) or Lancaster (1990).

28. For an elaboration of these points, see Flinn and Heckman (1982b).

29. It should be noted that in a general equilibrium framework the parameters of the state unemployment regression function would be related to those in the mean duration function, i.e., the γ's would be explicit functions of the π's. Indeed, if instead of using the state unemployment rate one had used the average duration of unemployment in the state, the γ's would equal the respective π's. I will return to this point in the discussion of equilibrium search models below.

30. Marschak's (1949) distinction between variables and parameters is particularly relevant for the following discussion.

31. Actually, they conduct the analysis for individuals grouped by duration and argue that the constant reservation wage assumption is more valid for those with longer durations. Recall that in the limit the finite horizon reservation wage converges to the stationary reservation wage.

32. Lancaster and Chesher do not present the elasticities of w^* and h with respect to the mean of the wage offer distribution because those elasticities depend on the wage offer mean which is unmeasured. One can determine the absolute derivatives from the available information. They are

$$\frac{\partial w^*}{\partial \mu} : 0 \le \frac{w^* - b}{x - b} \le 1$$

$$\frac{\partial h}{\partial \mu} : pf\left(w^*\right)\frac{x - w^*}{x - b} \ge 0$$

Notice that both of those effects are signed.

33. $E\left(w \mid w > w^*\right) = \left(\dfrac{\alpha + 1}{\alpha + 2}\right) w^*$

34. For further discussion see Flinn and Heckman (1982a) and Wolpin (1987).

35. Blau (1991), Flinn and Heckman (1982a), Stern (1990), Van den Berg (1990), and Wolpin (1987) are other examples.

36. The length of eligibility varies in Engberg's data, but it is unclear whether, as in Meyer's data, it changes during any individual's actual unemployment spell.

37. Engberg also allows for the offer probability to be chosen optimally, i.e. for individuals to choose their search intensity at each duration. We ignore this complication for ease of exposition. Modeling search intensity in this way also enables Engberg to separately identify a value of leisure parameter and a (marginal) search cost parameter.

38. See Eckstein and Wolpin (1989) for a discussion of other estimation methods.

39. While one can choose any order statistic $w_{(K)}$ as a consistent estimate of the reservation wage as long as K/N is small, where N is the sample size, the choice must be made before observing the data. Given measurement error in wages, even if the reservation wage estimate obtained from a higher order statistic is consistent, other parameters that rely on the reservation wage estimate will in general not be consistent.

40. Sample variation in benefit exhaustion dates could also explain spikes.

41. See Rust (1991) for an example of this type of comparison in a different substantive context.

42. Another possibility is to solicit subjective judgments about the probability of receiving an offer and about the wage offer distribution. Although this proposal raises serious issues concerning survey questionnaire design, it would seem to me to be an avenue worth exploring. See Manski (1991) for a recent discussion of the value of subjective data.

43. They do not report the distribution of the reported reservation wage or of its difference from the optimal reservation wage. The evidence certainly would be more compelling if it were also true that a large proportion of the players were close to the correct reservation wage.

44. See for example Cox and Oaxaca (1989).

45. Experimentally generated data would differ in this way from data obtained by Monte Carlo experiments.

46. Diamond (1971), Rothschild (1973), Burdett and Judd (1983), Albrecht and Axell (1984), Rob (1985), Pissarides (1990), and Mortensen and Pissarides (1991) are examples.

47. The dividend, because it is invariant to employment state, does not affect the reservation wage.

48. This assumption is the only significant deviation from the original Albrecht and Axell model.

49. For a more general proof of existence than found in Eckstein and Wolpin, see Mortensen (1990).

50. It is unclear whether the solution to (39) is unique.

51. The model also generates an equilibrium unemployment rate given by

$$u = \sum_{j=0}^{n} \frac{\tau \beta_j \left[p\gamma^j + (1-p) \right]}{1 - (1-\tau)\left[p\gamma^j + (1-p) \right]}.$$

Notice that it depends on exactly the same parameters as does the duration density and hazard functions. Thus, it is clear why in the system given by (27) the assumption that $\gamma_1 = 0$ would be inappropriate.

52. From (40), $p(1 - \gamma^j)$ is identified for all j.

53. In a linear system this restriction would be necessary but not sufficient. In a non-linear system, it is neither.

54. With accepted wage data the functional form restriction imposed on the z_j's can be relaxed.

55. Mortensen (1990) extends the Albrecht and Axell model to allow for jobs that do not necessarily last forever. This formulation yields a continuous equilibrium wage offer distribution. van den Berg and Ridder (1993) empirically implement that model.

56. Among other studies where three state models have been estimated, although not motivated by the distinctness issue, are Burdett *et al.* (1984), Mortensen and Neumann (1984), and van den Berg (1990).

57. A more complete formalization of a job search model with on-the-job search behavior can be found in Burdett (1978). Also, see Wolpin (1992) and below.

58. Topel offers a different interpretation of using behavioral modeling. Specifically, he states as an alternative 'to explicitly model the mobility decisions that underlie the selection bias, in which case standard sample selection corrections (e.g. Heckman, 1976) might be applied. With this strategy, identification relies crucially on distributional assumptions (wage offers must be normally distributed), as well as on other strong restrictions.' With such a strategy, however, one is not necessarily restricted to selection mechanisms (that is, mobility choices) that are consistent with any optimizing behavioral model.

59. It is also assumed that a quit precludes a layoff.

60. Wolpin also assumes that wages are measured with error with the observed wage and the measured wage being proportional up to an iid normal measurement error.

61. An individual was defined to be unemployed if he did not work at least thirty hours per week in each week of the calendar quarter. A better description of this state would be non-full-time employment.

62. There is some slippage between the time an individual graduates and the beginning of the employment clock, which is the first week of the calendar quarter following graduation.

63. The earliest examples of obtaining tractability essentially through small choice sets and state spaces are those of Gotz and McCall (1984) and Wolpin (1984).

64. Miller formulates an occupational choice model as a multi-armed bandit problem. The method he develops for tractably solving (employing the Gittens index) and estimating that model, accommodating as it does a large choice set and serial correlation in wages, is generalizable to problems with the same structure. Its main drawback is that the assumption in such problems of independence across arms may be too restrictive over a broad range of economic problems. For example, it would be inapplicable to the occupational choice model we consider if work experience in one occupation affects

productivity in another occupation. Pakes considers an optimal stopping problem (whether or not to renew a patent) in which serially correlated unobservables enter the reward function additively. While the distributional assumptions that make the solution of the dynamic programming problem tractable are specific to the particular problem, and thus not generally transportable to other stopping problems, Pakes demonstrated the feasibility of incorporating serial correlation into the estimation of discrete choice dynamic programming models.

65. There is a direct analogy to nested logit, but without its usual implied sequential decision-making interpretation. Even in the non-nested case, the independence of irrelevant alternatives axiom does not hold in the dynamic setting because augmenting the choice set must affect the valuation attached to all choices.

66. For a brief description of Manski's approach see Eckstein and Wolpin (1989).

REFERENCES

Abraham, K. G. and H. S. Farber (1987): 'Job Duration, Seniority, and Earnings.' *American Economic Review,* **77(3)**, 278–297.

Albrecht, J. W. and B. Axell (1984): 'An Equilibrium Model of Search Employment.' *Journal of Political Economy,* **92(4)**, 824–840.

Altonji, J. and R. Shakatko (1987): 'Do Wages Rise with Job Seniority?' *Review of Economic Studies,* **54**, 437–459.

Atkinson, A. B. and J. Micklewright (1992): 'Unemployment Compensation and Labor Market Transitions: A Critical Review.' *Journal of Economic Literature,* **29(4)**, 1679–1727.

Bellman, Richard (1957): *Dynamic Programming.* Princeton: Princeton University Press.

Blau, D. M. (1991): 'Search for Non-Wage Job Characteristics: A Test of the Reservation Wage Hypothesis.' *Journal of Labor Economics,* **9(2)**, 186–205.

Blau, D. M., and P. K. Robbins (1990): 'Job Search Outcomes for the Employed and Unemployed.' *Journal of Political Economy,* **98(3)**, 637–655.

Burdett, K. and K. Judd (1983): 'Equilibrium Price Dispersion.' *Econometrica,* **51(4)**, July, 955–970.

Burdett, K. and D. T. Mortensen (1978): 'Labor Supply under Uncertainty.' In R. Ehrenberg (ed.), *Research in Labor Economics,* Vol. 2 JAI Press, Greenwich, Conn., pp. 109–157

Burdett, K., N. M. Kiefer, D. T. Mortensen, and G. R. Neumann (1984): 'Earnings, Unemployment, and the Allocation of Time Over Time.' *Review of Economic Studies,* **51**, 559–578.

Burgess, P. L. and J. L. Kingston (1977): 'Impact of Unemployment Insurance Benefits on Reemployment Success.' *Industrial and Labor Relations Review,* **30(3)**, July, 25–31.

Christensen, B. J. and N. M. Kiefer (1992): 'Measurement Error in the Prototypical Search Model.' New York University, mimeo.

Clark, K. B. and L. H. Summers (1982): 'Unemployment Insurance and Labor Market Transitions.' In M. N. Baily (ed.), *Workers, Jobs, and Inflation.* The Brookings Institution, Washington D. C., pp. 279–324.

Classen, K. P. (1977): 'The Effect of Unemployment Insurance on the Duration of Employment and Subsequent Earnings.' *Industrial and Labor Relations Review,* **30(8)**, 438–444.

Cox, J. C. and R. L. Oaxaca (1989): 'Laboratory Experiments with a Finite Horizon Job Search Model.' *Journal of Risk and Uncertainty,* **2**, 301–330.

Devine, T. J. and N. M. Kiefer (1991): *Empirical Labor Economics.* Oxford University Press, New York.

Diamond, P. (1971): 'A Model of Price Adjustment.' *Journal of Economic Theory,* **3**, 156–168.

Ehrenberg, R. G. and R. L. Oaxaca (1976): 'Unemployment Insurance, Duration of Unemployment, and Subsequent Wage Gain.' *American Economic Review,* **66**, 754–766.

Eckstein, Z. and K. I. Wolpin (1989): 'The Specification and Estimation of Dynamic Stochastic Discrete Choice Models.' *Journal of Human Resources,* **24(4)**, 562–598.

Eckstein, Z. and K. I. Wolpin (1990): 'Estimating a Market Equilibrium Search Model from Panel Data on Individuals.' *Econometrica,* **54(4)**, 783–808.

Eckstein, Z. and K. I. Wolpin (1992): 'Duration to First Job Search and the Return to Schooling: Estimates from a Search-Matching Model.' University of Minnesota, mimeo.

Ellwood, D. (1982): 'Teenage Unemployment: Temporary Blemish or Permanent Scar?' In R. Freeman and D. Wise (eds.), *The Youth Labor Market Problem.* University of Chicago Press, Chicago, pp. 349–390.

Engberg, J. B. (1991): 'The Impact of Unemployment Benefits on Job Search: Structural Unobserved Heterogeneity and Spurious Spikes.' Carnegie Mellon University, mimeo.

Feldstein, M. and J. Poterba (1984): 'Unemployment Insurance and Reservation Wages.' *Journal of Public Economics,* **23**, 141–167.

Flinn, C. and J. J. Heckman (1982a): 'New Methods for Analyzing Structural Models of Labor Force Dynamics.' *Journal of Econometrics,* **18**, 115–168.

Flinn, C. and J. J. Heckman (1982b): 'Models for the Analysis of Labor Force Dynamics.' *Advances in Econometrics,* **1**, 35–95.

Flinn, C. and J. J. Heckman (1983): 'Are Unemployment and Out of the Labor Force Behaviorally Distinct Labor Force States?' *Journal of Labor Economics,* **1(1)**, 28–42.

Gonul, F. (1992): 'New Evidence on Whether Unemployment and Out-of-the-Labor Force are Distinct States.' *Journal of Human Resources,* **27(2)**, forthcoming.

Geweke, John, Robert Slonim, and Gary Zarkin (1992): 'Econometric Solution Methods for Dynamic Discrete Choice Problems.' mimeo, University of Minnesota.

Gotz, G. and J. J. McCall (1984): 'Estimating the Stay/Leave Decisions in a Sequential Decision Making Model.' Report R-3028-AF, the RAND Corporation, Santa Monica, Calfornia.

Ham, J. C. and S. Rea (1987): 'Unemployment Insurance and Male Unemployment Duration in Canada.' *Journal of Labor Economics,* **5(3)**, 325–353.

Heckman, J. J. (1976): 'The Common Structure of Statistical Models of Truncation, Sample Selection and Limited Dependent Variables and a Simple Estimator for Such Models.' *Annals of Economics and Social Measurement,* **5**, 475–492.

Heckman, J. J. and B. Singer (1984): 'A Method for Minimizing the Impact of Distributional Assumptions in Econometric Models for Duration Data.' *Econometrica,* **52**, March, 271–320.

Heckman, J. J. and J. R. Walker (1990): 'The Relationship between Wages and Income and the Timing and Spacing of Births: Evidence from Swedish Longitudinal Data.' *Econometrica,* **58(6)**, 1411–1442.

Hotz, Joseph V. and Robert A. Miller (1993): 'Conditional Choice Probabilities and the Estimation of Dynamic Programming Models.' *Review of Economic Studies,* **60**, 497–530.

Hotz, V. Joseph, Robert A. Miller, Seth Sanders, and Jeffrey Smith (1994): 'A Simulation Estimator for Dynamic Models of Discrete Choice.' *Review of Economic Studies,* **61**, 265–290.

Kahn, L. M. (1978): 'The Returns to Job Search: A Test of Two Models.' *The Review of Economics and Statistics.* **60**. November. 496–503.

Kalbfleish, J. and R. Prentice (1980): *The Statistical Analysis of Failure Time Data*. Wiley, New York.

Kasper, H. (1967): 'The Asking Price of Labor and the Duration of Unemployment.' *Review of Economics and Statistics*, **49(2)**, 165–172.

Keane, Michael P., and Kenneth I. Wolpin (1994): 'The Solution and Estimation of Discrete Choice Dynamic Programming Models by Simulation and Interpolation: Monte Carlo Evidence,' *Review of Economics and Statistics*, **76(4)**, 648–672.

Keane, Michael P., and Kenneth I. Wolpin (1994): 'The Career Decisions of Young Men.' mimeo, New York University.

Kiefer, N. M. (1988). 'Economic Duration Data and Hazard Functions.' *Journal of Economic Literature*, **26(2)**, 646–679.

Kiefer, N. M. and G. R. Neumann (1979): 'An Empirical Job Search Model with a Test of the Constant Reservation Wage Hypothesis.' *Journal of Political Economy*, **87**, 89–107.

Kum, J. (1992): 'Dynamic Search of Non-employed Individuals.' University of Minnesota, mimeo.

Lancaster, T. (1985): 'Simultaneous Equations Models in Applied Search Theory.' *Journal of Econometrics, Annals*, **28(1)**, 113–126.

Lancaster, T. (1990): *The Econometric Analysis of Transition Data*. Cambridge University Press, New York.

Lancaster, T. and A. Chesher (1983): 'An Econometric Analysis of Reservation Wages.' *Econometrica*, **51(6)**, 1661–1776.

Lancaster, T. and S. Nickell (1980): 'The Analysis of Reemployment Probabilities for the Unemployed.' *Journal of the Royal Statistical Society A*, **143**, 2, 141–165.

Lumsdaine, R., James Stock and David Wise (1992): 'Three Models of Retirement: Computational Complexity vs. Predictive Validity.' in D. Wise (ed.), *Topics in the Economics of Aging*, Chicago: University of Chicago.

Manski, Charles (1988): 'Path Utility Analysis of Dynamic Choice.' SSRI Working Paper #8805, Madison: University of Wisconsin.

Manski, Charles (1991): 'Adolescent Econometricians: How Do Youth Infer the Returns to Schooling?' University of Wisconsin, mimeo.

McFadden, Daniel (1973): 'Conditional Logit Analysis of Qualitative Choice Behavior,' in P. Zarembka (ed.), *Frontiers of Econometrics*, Academic Press: New York.

Marschak, J. (1949): 'Economic Measurement for Policy and Prediction.' *Econometrica*, **17**, 125–144.

McCall, J. J. (1970): 'The Economics of Information and Job Search.' *Quarterly Journal of Economics*, **84(1)**, 113–126.

Meyer, B. D. (1990): 'Unemployment Insurance and Unemployment Spells.' *Econometrica*, **58**, 757–782.

Miller, R. (1984): 'Job Matching and Occupational Choice.' *Journal of Political Economy*, **92**, April, 1086–1120.

Mortensen, D. T. (1970): 'Job Search, the Duration of Unemployment, and the Phillips Curve.' *American Economic Review*, **60(5)**, 505–517.

Mortensen, D. T. (1977): 'Unemployment Insurance and the Labor Supply Decision.' *Industrial and Labor Relations Review*, **30(3)**, 505–517.

Mortensen, D. T. (1986): 'Job Search and Labor Market Analysis.' In O. C. Ashenfelter and R. Layard (eds.), *Handbook of Labor Economics*, Vol. II. North Holland, Amsterdam, pp. 849–919.

Mortensen, D. T. (1990): 'Equilibrium Wage Distributions: A Synthesis.' in J. Hartog and G. Ridder (eds.), *Panel Data and Labor Market Studies*. North-Holland: New York, pp. 279–296.

Mortensen D. T. and G. R. Neumann (1984): 'Choice or Chance? A Structural Interpretation of Individual Labor Market Histories.' In G. R. Neumann and W. Westergaard-Nielsen (eds.), *Studies in Labor Market Dynamics*. Springer-Verlag, Heidelberg, pp. 98–131.

Mortensen D. T. and C. A. Pissarides (1991): 'Job Creation and Job Destruction in the Theory of the Unemployed.' Northwestern University, mimeo.

Newton, F. and H. Rosen (1979): 'Unemployment Insurance, Income Taxation, and the Duration of Unemployment: Evidence from Georgia.' *Southern Economic Journal*, **45**, 773–784.

Pakes, A. (1987): 'Patents as Options: Some Estimates of the Value of Holding European Patent Stocks.' *Econometrica*, **54**, 755–784.

Pissarides, C. A. (1990): *Equilibrium Unemployment Theory*, Oxford: Blackwell.

Rob, R. (1985): 'Equilibrium Price Distributions.' *Review of Economic Studies*, **52**, 487–504.

Rothschild, M. (1973): 'Models of Market Organization with Imperfect Information: A Survey.' *Journal of Political Economy*, **81**, 1283–1308.

Rust, J. (1987): 'Optimal Replacement of GMC Bus Engines: An Empirical Model of Harold Zurcher.' *Econometrica*, **55**, 999–1035.

Rust, J. (1991): 'Estimation of Dynamic Structural Models: Problems and Prospects.' University of Wisconsin, mimeo.

Rust, J. (forthcoming): 'Structural Estimation of Markov Decision Processes.' in R. Engle and D. McFadden (eds.), *Handbook of Econometrics*, Vol. 4, North Holland: Amsterdam.

Schotter, A. and Y. M. Braunstein (1981): 'Economic Search: An Experimental Study.' *Economic Inquiry*, **19**, January, 1–25.

Stern, S. (1990): 'Estimating a Simultaneous Search Model.' *Journal of Labor Economics*, **7**, 348–369.

Stern, S. (1991): 'Approximate Solutions to Stochastic Dynamic Programming Problems.' mimeo, University of Virginia.

Stock, James and David Wise (1990): 'Pensions, the Option Value of Work and Retirement,' *Econometrica*, **58**, 1151–1180.

Topel, R. (1984): 'Equilibrium Earnings, Turnover, and Unemployment: New Evidence.' *Journal of Labor Economics*, **2**, 500–522.

Topel, R. (1991): 'Specific Capital, Mobility, and Wages: Wages Rise with Job Seniority.' *Journal of Political Economy*, **99(1)**, 145–176.

van den Berg, G. J. (1990): 'Nonstationarity in Job Search Theory.' *Review of Economic Studies*, **57**, 255–277.

van den Berg, G. J. (1991): 'The Effect of an Increase of the Rate of Arrival of Job Offers on the Duration of Unemployment.' Groningen University, mimeo.

van den Berg, G. J. and G. Ridder (1993): 'An Empirical Equilibrium Search Model of the Labour Market.' Vrije Universiteit, Amsterdam, mimeo.

Welch, F. (1977): 'What Have We Learned from Empirical Studies of Unemployment Insurance?' *Industrial and Labor Relations Review*, **30(3)**, July, 451–461.

Wolpin, K. I. (1984): 'An Estimable Dynamic Stochastic Model of Fertility and Child Mortality.' *Journal of Political Economy*, **92**, 852–874.

Wolpin, K. I. (1987): 'Estimating a Structural Search Model: The Transition from School to Work.' *Econometrica*, **55(4)** 801–818.

Wolpin, K. I. (1992): 'The Determinants of Black-White Differences in Early Employment Careers: Search, Layoffs, Quits, and Endogenous Wage Growth.' *Journal of Political Economy*, **110**, 535–560.

APPENDIX A

Numerical Solution Algorithm

Numerical solution of the dynamic program is necessary for estimation. Because of the size of the problem, a number of approximations were necessary. It is therefore useful to provide the details of the algorithm. The dynamic program is solved backwards from T for a given set of parameter values, $b, c, \bar{n}, \delta$, for a given $w_0(SK, GK)$ function and given P_1, P_2, P_3, and P_4 functions, and for a given distribution of u. The algorithm proceeds as follows:

1. Compute V_T^Q, V_T^L and V_t^E, the latter for values of $u = \underline{u}, \underline{u} + k, \underline{u} + 2k$, $\ldots, 0, \ldots, \bar{u} - 2k, \bar{u} - k, \bar{u}$, where k is a scalar which determines the number of separate u values used in the computation of V_T^E, $\underline{u}$ is a lower bound for u and $\bar{u}$ is an upper bound for u. In practice, the distribution of u is discretized by assuming an underlying i.i.d. normal distribution $(N(0, \sigma^2))$ and calculating mass points at each of the u-values given above beginning from the interval $(-\infty, \underline{u})$. The last mass point at $\underline{u}$ is calculated from the interval $(\bar{u} - k, \infty)$. The number of intervals is held constant as σ changes by multiplying each u value by σ, i.e. $\underline{u}\sigma, (\underline{u} + k)\sigma$, etc. The literal interpretation of the discretization procedure is that wages take on only $\dfrac{\bar{u} - \underline{u}}{k} + 1$ values.

V_T^E must be computed for each of the possible $u \times GK \times SK$ combinations and V_T^L for two values depending on whether unemployment compensation benefits have been exhausted. V_T^Q takes on only one value. The reservation values at T, namely $u_T^{*Q}(SK, GK), u_T^{*L}(n, 0, GK), u_T^{*R}(n, SK, GK)$ and $u_T^{*N}(u, SK, GK)$ are calculated as the value of u closest to the solution to (4) (in distance between value functions) from among the discretized values.

2. The value functions at T $-$ 1 are computed from

$$V_{T-1}^Q(n, GK) = b + \delta \Big\{ P_1(n + 1, GK)$$

$$\times \left[V_T^Q \sum_{\underline{u}}^{u_t^{*Q}(0,GK)} f(u) + \sum_{u_t^{*Q}(0,GK)}^{\bar{u}} V_T^E(u, 0, GK) f(u) \right]$$

$$+ \big(1 - P_1(n + 1, GK)\big) V_T^Q \Big\} \tag{A.1}$$

where $u_T^{*Q-}(0,GK)$ is the value of u one below $u_T^{*Q}(0,GK)$ As (A.1) indicates an offer of $u_T^{*Q}(0,GK)$ is accepted while an offer of $u_T^{*Q-}(0,GK)$ is rejected.

$$V_{T-1}^L(n,SK,GK) = b + c(n) + \delta\{P_1(n+1,GK)$$

$$\times \left[V_T^L(n+1)\sum_{\underline{u}}^{u_T^{\circ L-}(n+1,GK)} f(u) + \sum_{u_T^{\circ L}(n+1,GK)}^{\bar{u}} V_T^E(u,0,G)f(u)\right]$$

$$+ P_4(n+1,SK)\left[V_T^L(n+1)\sum_{\underline{u}}^{u_T^{\circ R-}(n+1,SK,GK)} f(u) + \sum_{u_T^{\circ R}(n+1,SK,GK)}^{\bar{u}} V_T^E(u,SK,GK)f(u)\right]$$

$$+ \left(1 - P_1(n+1,GK) - P_4(n+1,SK)\right)V_T^L(n+1,SK,GK)\} \qquad (A.2)$$

where $u_T^{*L-}(n+1,GK)$ is the value of u one below $u_T^{*L}(n+1,GK)$. As with the quit value function an offer of $u_T^{*L}(n+1,GK)$ is accepted as is a recall offer of $u_T^{*R}(n+1,SK,GK)$.

$$V_{T-1}^E(u,SK,GK) = w_0(SK,GK)e^u + \delta\left\{ P_2(GK+1)\left[V_T^Q\sum_{\underline{u}}^{u_{,}^{v}(0,GK+1)} f(u)\right.\right.$$

$$\left.\left. + \sum_{u_{,}^{v}(0,GK+1)}^{\bar{u}} V_T^E(u',0,GK+1)f(u')\right] + \left(1 - P_2(GK+1)\right)V_T^Q \right\}$$

$$\text{if } u < u_T^{*Q}(SK+1,GK+1)$$

$$V_{T-1}^E(u,SK,GK) = w_0(SK,GK)e^u + \delta\{P_2(GK+1)(1 - P_3(SK+1))$$

$$\times \left[V_T^E(u,SK+1,GK+1)\sum_{\underline{u}}^{u_{,}^{v}(u,SK+1,GK+1)} f(u) + \sum_{u_{,}^{v}(0,SK+1,GK+1)}^{\bar{u}} V_T^E(u',0,GK+1)f(u')\right]$$

$$+ P_2(GK+1)(P_3(SK+1))\left[V_T^L(0)\sum_{\underline{u}}^{u_{,}^{v}(0,GK+1)} f(u) + \sum_{u_{,}^{v}(0,GK)}^{\bar{u}} V_T^E(u',0,GK+1)f(u')\right]$$

$$+ \left(1 - P_2(GK+1)\right)P_3(SK+1)V_T^L(0)$$

$$+ \left(1 - P_2(GK+1)\right)(1 - P_3(SK+1))V_T^E(u,SK+1,GK+1)\}$$

$$\text{if } u \geq u_T^{*Q}(SK+1,GK+1). \qquad (A.3)$$

$u_T^{*N-}(u,SK+1,GK+1)$ is the value of u one below $u_T^{*N}(u,SK+1,GK+1)$ which again is an acceptable offer.

V_{T-1}^Q must be calculated $n \times GK$ times, V_{T-1}^Q $n \times SK \times GK$ times, and V_{T-1}^E $u \times SK \times GK$ times. $u_{T-1}^{*Q}(n, SK, GK), u_{T-1}^{*L}(n, SK, GK), u_{T-1}^{*R}(n, SK, GK)$ and $u_{T-1}^{*N}(u, SK, GK)$ are calculated as the closest values to the solution to (4).

3. Continue solving backwards for period $T - 2$, $T - 3$, ..., 1 using the value functions given by (3). The complete solution yields values of $u_t^{*Q}(n, SK, GK), u_t^{*L}(n, SK, GK), u_t^{*R}(n, SK, GK)$, and $u_t^{*N}(u, SK, GK)$ for all $t = 1, ..., T$.

The estimation is carried out using quarterly observations. T represents the entire working lifetime, say about 160 quarters. The state space at period T is thus of the order $\dfrac{(160)(161)}{2} \times \left(\dfrac{\bar{u} - \underline{u}}{k} + 1 \right)$ which for any reasonable size discretization of u is computationally intractable as an estimation problem, i.e. where the dynamic program must be simulated thousands of times. To make the problem tractable, it was assumed that the individual approximates the solution by optimizing over different period lengths during the backwards solution using longer period lengths for the more distant future value functions.

Rather than discuss the general strategy, it is more illuminating to present the solution as actually implemented. The generalization is then obvious. Figure A.1 depicts the temporal scheme of the optimization problem.

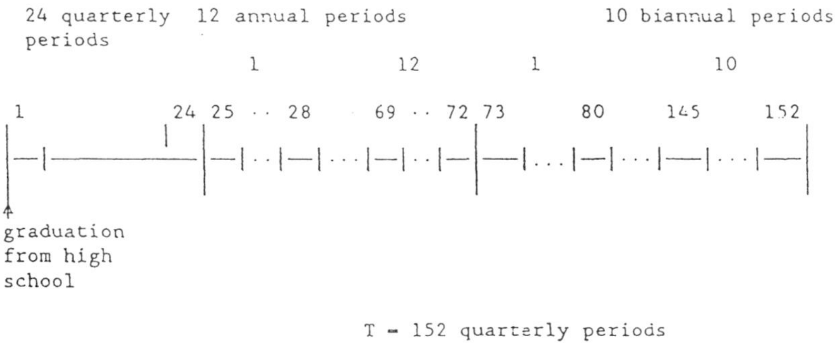

```
24 quarterly   12 annual periods                    10 biannual periods
periods
                    1              12        1                 10

1                24 25  ·· 28    69 ·· 72 73        80      145         152
|—|——————————————|—|··|—|···|—|··|—|————|...|—|···|—|···|—|
|
↑
graduation
from high
school


                        T - 152 quarterly periods

                              FIGURE A.1
```

From quarter 152 through quarter 73 the individual acts as if optimization occurs over two-year periods (eight quarters per decision period), from quarter 72 through quarter 25 over one-year periods (four quarters per decision period), and from quarter 24 through quarter 1 over quarterly periods. Of course the discount factor (δ), the per-period value of leisure (b), the level of unemployment compensation, the probability functions (P_1, P_2, P_3, P_4) and the wage function must be appropriate to the period length. Details of these adjustments are provided below.

Now, after having solved the biannual period problem back to period one of the ten biannual periods, i.e. quarters 77–84 it is necessary to convert the state variables, namely n, SK and GK, from biannual to annual units. Similarly, a conversion from annual to quarterly units is necessary at period one of the annual periods. However, the value functions are only calculated for biannual units of the state variables in the first case and for annual units in the second, and so it is necessary to use some interpolation method. The following regressions were used to perform the interpolation:

$$V^Q(n, GK) = \beta_1^Q + \beta_2^Q n + \beta_3^Q GK + \beta_4^Q n^2 + \beta_5^Q GK^2$$

$$V^L(n, SK, GK) = \beta_1^L + \beta_2^L n + \beta_3^L SK + \beta_4^L GK + \beta_5^L 1(n < \bar{n})$$

$$V^E(u, SK, GK) = \beta_1^E + \beta_2^E SK + \beta_3^E GK + \beta_4^E SK^2 + \beta_5^E GK^2$$

for each u from $\underline{u}$ to $\bar{u}$.

Adjustments for the discount factor, the value of leisure and the level of unemployment compensation are straightforward. The quarterly rate of interest is multiplied by four and eight, respectively, with the discount factor, $\delta = 1/(1 + r)$. The quarterly value of leisure is also multiplied by four and eight, respectively. The adjusted level of unemployment compensation depends on $\bar{n}$. Because $\bar{n}$ is set to 2, i.e. individuals are assumed to be eligible for unemployment compensation for two quarters (26 weeks), the level of unemployment compensation for both annual and biannual periods is 2-times the quarterly benefit level (c) and the duration is one period.

The probability functions would be straightforward to adjust if they were not dependent on state variables. To illustrate how this is handled, consider $P_1(n, GK)$. Let the quarterly $P_1(n, GK)$ be parameterized as

$$P_1^q(n, GK) = \frac{\exp(\alpha_0 + \alpha_1 n + \alpha_2 GK)}{1 + \exp(\alpha_0 + \alpha_1 n + \alpha_2 GK)} \text{ where } n \text{ and } GK \text{ are measured in}$$

quarters.

The annual $P_1(n, GK)$ is then given by

$$P_1^a(n, GK) = \left(\frac{A + B}{2}\right)$$

where n and GK are measured in years and where

$$A = 1 - (1 - X_a)^4, \qquad B = 1 - (1 - X_b)^4,$$

$$X_a = \frac{\exp(\alpha_0 + 4\alpha_1 n + 4\alpha_2 GK)}{1 + \exp(\alpha_0 + 4\alpha_1 n + 4\alpha_2 GK)},$$

$$X_b = \frac{\exp(\alpha_0 + 4\alpha_1(n+1) + 4\alpha_2(GK+1))}{1 + \exp(\alpha_0 + 4\alpha_1(n+1) + 4\alpha_2(GK+1))}.$$

The biannual conversion uses eight instead of four in the formulas for A, B, X_a and X_b. Note that A and B are simply the probabilities of receiving an offer any time during the annual or biannual period based on the quarterly probability, i.e. ignoring state variable $p_1^a = p_1^q + (1 - P_1^q) p_1^q + (1 - p_1^q)^2 p_1^q + (1 - p_1^q)^3 p_1^q = 1 - (1 - p_1^q)^4$. But, because the state variable based on quarterly units may change over the annual period, an average of the annual probability at the smallest and largest possible values of the state variable over the annual period is used. Exactly analogous representations hold for P_2, P_3, and P_4.

A similar issue arises with the wage function because it too depends on state variables. Defining the wage function on a quarterly basis implies the annual wage may take on a number of values depending on how the levels of specific and general experience change over the four quarters. Consider the quarterly wage function

$$\ell n \, w^q = a_0 + a_1, GK + a_2 SK + a_3 GK^2 + a x SK^2;$$

GK and SK are measured in quarters.
The conversion of the quarterly wage to an annual wage is performed as follows:

a.   when $GK = SK = 0, w^a = 4\exp\left(\ell n \, w^q (GK = 0, SK = 0)\right)$

b.   when $GK \geq 1, SK = 0, w^a = \sum_{i=1}^{4} \exp\left(\ell n \, w^q (4GK - 1 + i, SK = 0)\right)$

c.   when $GK \geq 1, SK \geq 1, w^a = \sum_{i=1}^{4} \exp\left(\ell n \, w^q (4GK - 1 + i, 4SK - 1 + i)\right).$

(A. 7)

Similarly, over the biannual period the sum is over eight quarters rather than four. Thus, the assumption is that over the annual period experience is continuously (quarterly) accumulated and the annual wage is just the sum of the quarterly wages.

APPENDIX B

The Likelihood Function

As discussed in the text, it is only necessary to consider a representative cycle because of the i.i.d. assumption. In addition, recall that the unemployment spell duration is independent of subsequent employment spells within any cycle. Therefore, the components of the likelihood function as in (61) can be separately considered. The details of the likelihood function will be presented for the first two cycles. Because, as will become evident, the number of multiple integrations (sums) required to evaluate the likelihood function is equal to the number of employer spells within a cycle, in estimation an observation is truncated at the point at which a third employer spell is begun, i.e. all future employer spells and all later cycles are ignored accounting correctly for entry into the third spell. Thus, at most triple integrations are required, and only for those individuals who have completed a second employer spell in a cycle.

First Cycle

Consider first an individual with a cycle 1 employment and wage profile $\left(d_1, e_1^1, e_2^1, e_3^1 > 0, \hat{w}_1^1, \hat{w}_2^1\right)$. Recall that, except for unemployment durations, superscripts refer to cycle and subscripts to employer spells. The probability of this event is

$$Pr\left(d_1, e_1^1, e_2^1, e_3^1 > 0, \hat{w}_1^1, \hat{w}_2^1,\right) = Pr\left(d_I\right) Pr\left(e_1^1, e_2^1, e_3^1 > 0, \hat{w}_1^1, \hat{w}_2^1,\right), \quad (B.\ 1)$$

because of the i.i.d. assumption. The probability of observing an unemployment duration of d_1 periods is

$$Pr\left(d_I\right) = \prod_{k=1}^{d_1} \left[P_1(k-1,0) \, Pr\left(u_k < u_k^{*Q}(k-1,0,0)\right) + \left(1 - P_1(k-1,0)\right)\right], \tag{B.\ 2}$$

where $d_1 = 1$ refers to a person who was unemployed for one period after leaving school. A person who receives a job offer and accepts it immediately upon leaving school has $d_1 = 0$ and is accounted for below. In each period the probability of remaining unemployed is the probability of receiving an offer and rejecting it plus the probability of not receiving an offer. The second component of (B1) is proportional to $Pr\left(e_1^1, e_2^1, e_3^1 > 0, v_1^1, v_2^1\right)$ where $v_1^1 = u_1^1 + \epsilon_1^1, v_2^1 = u_2^1 + \epsilon_2^1$ are vectors over the periods in each employment spell and the factor of proportionality is the Jacobian of the transformation which depends only on observed wages and so can be ignored in the estimation. Now,

$$Pr\left(e_1^1, e_2^1, e_3^1 > 0, v_1^1, v_2^1\right)$$

$$= \sum_{u_3^1} \sum_{u_2^1} \sum_{u_1^1} Pr\left(e_1^1, e_2^1, e_3^1 > 0, \big| u_1^1, u_2^1, u_3^1\right)$$

$$\times Pr\left(v_1^1, v_2^1 \big| u_1^1, u_2^1\right) Pr\left(u_1^1, u_2^1, u_3^1\right) du_1^1, du_2^1, du_3^1. \qquad \text{(B. 3)}$$

Because both the true wage distribution and the measurement error distribution are each independent over time and spells, one can write

$$Pr\left(v_1^1, v_2^1 \big| u_1^1, u_2^1\right) Pr\left(u_1^1, u_2^1, u_3^1\right)$$

$$= Pr\left(v_1^1 \big| u_1^1\right) Pr\left(v_2^1 \big| u_2^1\right) Pr\left(u_1^1\right) Pr\left(u_2^1\right) Pr\left(u_3^1\right). \qquad \text{(B. 4)}$$

where it is assumed that the conditional densities of v given u follow the approximate bivariate conditional normal,

$$Pr\left(v_i^1 \big| u_i^1\right) = \prod_{k=1}^{e_i^1} \Phi\left(\frac{v_{ik}^1 - \rho \frac{\sigma_v}{\sigma_u} u_i^1}{\sigma_v\left(1-\rho^2\right)^{\frac{1}{2}}}\right) \frac{1}{\sigma_v\left(1-\rho^2\right)^{\frac{1}{2}}} \frac{1}{(2\Pi)^{\frac{1}{2}}} \quad i = 1, 2 \qquad \text{(B. 5)}$$

and u_i^1 is a discretized approximation to a normal density as discussed in Appendix A.

It remains to characterize $Pr\left(e_1^1, e_2^1, e_3^1 > 0 \big| u_1^1, u_2^1, u_3^1\right)$. Letting $L_i^1 = 1$ if the individual was laid off from employment spell i (in cycle 1) and zero otherwise, and recalling that a new offer can arrive in the same period as a layoff,

$$Pr\left(e_1^1, e_2^1, e_3^1 > 0 \,\middle|\, u_1^1, u_2^1, u_3^1\right)$$

$$= P_1(d_1, 0)\left\{Pr\left(u_1^1 \geq \max\left(u_{d_1+1}^{*Q}(d_1, 0, 0), u_{d_1+2}^{*Q}(0, 1, 1),\right.\right.\right.$$

$$\left.\left.\left....,u_{d_1+e_1^1}^{*Q}\left(0, e_1^1-1, e_1^1-1\right)\right)\middle|u_1^1\right)\right\}$$

$$\times\left\{\prod_{k=d_1+2}^{d_1+e_1^1}\left[\left(1-P_3(k-d_1-1)\right)\left[P_2(k-d_1-1)\right.\right.\right.$$

$$Pr\left(u_k < u_k^{*N}\left(u_1^1, k-d_1-1, k-d_1-1\right)\middle|u_1^1\right)$$

$$\left.\left.\left.+\left(1-P_2(k-d_1-1)\right)\right]\right]\right\}$$

$$\times\left\{P_2\left(e_1^1\right)\left(1-P_3\left(e_1^1\right)\right)\left[Pr\left(u_2^1 \geq u_{d_1+e_1^1+1}^{*N}\left(u_1^1, e_1^1, e_1^1\right),\right.\right.\right.$$

$$u_2^1 \geq u_{d_1+e_1^1+1}^{*Q}\left(0, 0, e_1^1\right),$$

$$u_2^1 \geq u_{d_1+e_1^1+2}^{*Q}\left(0, 1, e_1^1+1\right),$$

$$\vdots$$

$$\left.\left.\left.u_2^1 \geq u_{d_1+e_1^1+e_2^1}^{*Q}\left(0, e_1^1-1, e_1^1+e_2^1-1\right)\middle|u_1^1, u_2^1\right)\right]\right\}^{1-L_1^1}$$

$$\times\left\{P_2\left(e_1^1\right)P_3\left(e_1^1\right)\left[Pr\left(u_2^1 \leq u_{d_1+e_1^1+1}^{*L}\left(0, e_1^1, e_1^1\right),\right.\right.\right.$$

$$u_2^1 \geq u_{d_1+e_1^1+2}^{*Q}\left(0, 1, e_1^1+1\right),$$

$$\vdots$$

$$\left.\left.\left.u_2^1 \geq u_{d_1+e_1^1+e_2^1}^{*Q}\left(0, e_2^1-1, e_1^1+e_2^1-1\right)\middle|u_2^1\right)\right]\right\}^{L_1^1}$$

$$\times\left\{\prod_{k=d_1+e_1^1+2}^{d_1+e_1^1+e_2^1}\left(1-P_3(k-d_1-e_1^1-1)\right)\left[P_2(k-d_1-e_1^1-1)\right.\right.$$

$$Pr\left(u_k < u_k^{*N}\left(u_2^1, k-d_1-e_1^1-1, k-d_1-1\right)\middle|u_2^1\right)$$

$$\left.\left.+\left(1-P_2(k-d_1-e_1^1-1)\right)\right]\right\}$$

$$\times\left\{P_2\left(e_1^1+e_2^1\right)\left(1-P_3\left(e_2^1\right)\right)\left[Pr\left(u_3^1 \geq \max\left(u_{d_1+e_1^1+e_2^1+1}^{*N}\left(u_2^1, e_2^1, e_1^1+e_2^1\right),\right.\right.\right.\right.$$

$$\left.\left.\left.\left.u_{d_1+e_1^1+e_2^1+1}^{*Q}\left(0, 0, e_1^1+e_2^1\right)\right)\middle|u_2^1, u_3^1\right)\right]\right\}^{1-L_2^1}$$

$$\times\left\{P_2\left(e_1^1+e_2^1\right)P_3\left(e_2^1\right)\left[Pr\left(u_3^1 \geq u_{d_1+e_1^1+e_2^1+1}^{*Q}\left(0, e_2^1, e_1^1+e_2^1\right)\middle|u_3^1\right)\right]\right\}^{L_2^1}.$$

$$(B.6)$$

Recall that the case of immediate employment ($d_1 < 0$) is incorporated into (B.6) rather than into (B.2). Because $e_3 > 0$ this individual is not followed into subsequent cycles.

Next, consider an individual who completed two employment spells and then entered cycle 2, i.e. became unemployed. For this individual $Pr\left(e_1^1, e_2^1, e_3^1 > 0 \mid u_1^1, u_2^1, u_3^1\right)$ is given by the same terms in (B.6) except for the last two which are replaced by the terms

$$\left\{P_3\left(e_2^1\right)\left[P_2\left(e_1^1+e_2^1\right)Pr\left(u < u_{d_1+e_1^1+e_2^1+1}^{*L}\left(0,e_2^1,e_1^1+e_2^1\right)\right)+\left(1-P_2\left(e_1^1+e_2^1\right)\right)\right]\right\}^{L_2^1}$$

$$\left\{\left(1-P_3\left(e_2^1\right)\right)\left[P_2\left(e_1^1+e_2^1\right)\left[Pr\left(u < u_{d_1+e_1^1+e_2^1+1}^{*N}\left(u_2^1,e_2^1,e_1^1+e_2^1\right),\right.\right.\right.\right.$$

$$u_2^1 < u_{d_1+e_1^1+e_2^1+1}^{*Q}\left(0,e_2^1,e_1^1+e_2^1\right)\Big| u_2^1\Big)$$

$$+Pr\left(u \ge u_{d_1+e_1^1+e_2^1+1}^{*N}\left(u_2^1,e_2^1,e_1^1+e_2^1\right),\right.$$

$$u < u_{d_1+e_1^1+e_2^1+1}^{*Q}\left(0,0,e_1^1+e_2^1\right)\Big| u_2^1\Big)\Big]$$

$$+\left(1-P_2\left(e_1^1+e_2^1\right)\right)Pr\left(u_2^1 < u_{d_1+e_1^1+e_2^1+1}^{*Q}\left(0,e_2^1,e_1^1+e_2^1\right)\Big| u_2^1\right)\Big]\right\}^{1-L_2^1}$$

$$(B.7)$$

The characterization of the probability statement for an individual with only one complete employment spell before entering the second cycle is obvious as is the characterization for an individual who never became employed.

Index

Printed in the USA/Agawam, MA
August 29, 2013

579497.005